HIDDEN HISTORY
of
KINSLEY

Joan K. Weaver and William Floyd Wolfgang

THE History PRESS

Published by The History Press
An imprint of Arcadia Publishing
Charleston, SC
www.historypress.com

First published 2025

Manufactured in the United States

ISBN 9781467158343

Library of Congress Control Number: 2025941484

Contents

Acknowledgements

We relied on the invaluable contributions of numerous sources and individuals to piece together this history. We are particularly indebted to the volumes prepared by Myrtle Richardson, Myron and Elizabeth Burr and the writers of the *Kinsley Mercury* and *Kinsley Graphic*. Their chronicles have been integral to the history we present.

Additionally, we are indebted to the support of all the citizens of Edwards County. Over the years, their generous donations have been instrumental in preserving the rich history of our community through the Edwards County Historical Society (ECHS) and its museum, including its collection of images. We wish to thank the ECHS for permission to publish the images. We are incredibly grateful to Julie Miller, the museum curator, for providing her expertise and access to that collection.

Similarly, the Kinsley Public Library has developed an extensive archive of local history files and images. In recent years, the library has been dedicated to making both the museum and library photos digitally accessible on its website. This close cooperation between the ECHS and the library proved instrumental in providing most of the images for this book. We also want to acknowledge the private citizens who have permitted us to use pictures from their personal collections. These include Edwin Carlson, Gary Jarvis, Stevenson Moffat, Lisa Sparke, John Wire Jr. and Rex Woods III.

We also owe a debt to two invaluable local historians: Rosetta Graff, retired Kinsley librarian and officer in the ECHS, and Ed Carlson, who possesses a wealth of knowledge and has generated many local history resources for the community. Additionally, we want to thank Judy Donley and Michelle Amaya, who provided a personal tour of the Edwards home, formerly Trail's End, and Gary Greene, who showed us through the Palace Theatre.

We extend our sincere thanks to Brian Gribben of the Special Collections at the Forsyth Library of Fort Hays State University and to Gwendolyn Sibley, the scholarly communication and copyright librarian of the Kansas State University Libraries, for their invaluable assistance in locating poems in the early literary magazines of their collections. We also express our gratitude to the Kansas State Historical Society for its assistance.

Finally, we are grateful to Dr. Mary Snow, William's longtime friend and mentor, who proofread the final manuscript.

Cast of Characters

This history contains numerous interesting and influential characters. Some do not remain confined to their given chapters but rather influence many aspects of Kinsley's history. So, with the spirit of the countless dramas Kinsley residents performed at the turn of the twentieth century, we have provided a "Cast of Characters" that lists the lead roles in this history. We hope our readers find this a helpful resource when exploring the *Hidden History of Kinsley*.

Gilmor Brown, a professional actor and director

Charlie Edwards, a poet, actor and theatrical producer

Lizzie Sellers Edwards, a socialite and arts supporter

Rufus Eugene Edwards, a merchant and brother of the county's namesake

Gustav Flohr, the proprietor of Kinsley's Opera House

Cora Lewis, "the Duchess," a writer and community leader

Tom Mairs, a Renaissance man

Lorin Raker, Kinsley's silent film star

Nell Woods, Kinsley's poet laureate

Prologue

The Kinsley Train Raid: 1878

Well before dawn on Sunday, January 27, 1878, snow silently coated the ground in Kinsley, Edwards County, Kansas, the halfway point between New York City and San Francisco. One of the few people awake at this deceptively calm hour was the railroad's night operator, Andy Kingkade. He was unaware that the squall that brought precipitation to the small but growing five-year-old community had just prevented a robbery about ten miles from town. Now the unsuccessful bandits were headed directly for Kinsley. The twenty-year-old watchman Kingkade sat behind the counter, customarily reviewing tickets for the two daily passenger trains, oblivious that he would be the last line of defense for several thousands of dollars in the railroad depot safe.

Lead desperado "Big Mike" Roarke ordered his five cronies to their positions as they assembled around the depot. Three stayed on the platform, and three went into the office. This time, they thought, the weather could not foil them. The recent snowstorm was the second time winter weather saved an unwary train from this same group of plunderers. Earlier in January, the criminal gang attempted to rob a train at Dodge City; they could not fail a third time. Adrenaline and hope must have run high among the bandits when it was confirmed that only one employee manned the office and platform.

When "Big Mike," his lieutenant Dave Rudabaugh and another bandit entered the railroad office, Kingkade greeted them with a routine "Good

An 1878 lithograph of Kinsley, Kansas. *Kansas State Historical Society*.

morning." In an instant, Kingkade understood it was a robbery upon seeing Roarke's unmistakable .45-caliber Sharps rifle. He reached for his pistol, ready to shoot Rudabaugh, but Roarke quipped, "I'll take that," and disarmed him. Defenseless and with his life on the line, Kingkade invented a story that the money in the safe had gone east on a previous train and that he could not open the safe even if he wanted to. He told the bandits that the key was in another building.

Roarke and Rudabaugh angrily forced Kingkade out of the office at gunpoint. At this precise moment, the passenger train approached, and so did William Blanchard, the editor of one of Kinsley's earliest newspapers, the *Kinsley Reporter*, and the proprietor of the Eureka House. Blanchard was on his way to have a morning chat with Kingkade. The outlaws attempted to restrain him as well. Taking advantage of Blanchard's inadvertent distraction, Kingkade jumped before the approaching train, narrowly escaping the cowcatcher. A gunshot followed.

On the other side of the engine, Kingkade alerted the engineer and conductor, and the gunfire began in earnest. Two robbers jumped into the engine as the others tried to take the express car. These bandits ordered the engineers under duress to start the train. At this point, everyone was armed, and somewhere between twenty-five to fifty shots were fired. As the train slowly pulled away from Kinsley, gun smoke and snow greeted the town's inhabitants, who filed into the streets. Amid this uproar, a group of townsmen pursued the train with a hand car. They found it stopped about two miles west of town after a thrilling chase. This pursuing posse fired at the six bandits, who were firmly mounted on their escape horses, but they would not make it far. At last, the raid on the passenger train at Kinsley had failed, and the newspapers near and far proclaimed night agent Andy Kingkade the town's hero.

This attack on the train was an assault on Kinsley's way of life. The first settlers founded the town in its current location because of the railroad. If the rail line became dangerous for business and personal travel, then everything was at risk. So, the authorities persecuted the robbers relentlessly and either imprisoned or killed them to prevent any further panic. The only desperado to escape relatively unpunished, after turning state's evidence and implicating his comrades, was "Dirty Dave" Rudabaugh. He continued his Wild West exploits with companions like Billy the Kid throughout the next decade. Meanwhile, as some residents of Kinsley prepared to protect themselves against future outlaws, others turned to making their home a better place.

WILD WEST SHOWS TO OPERA HOUSES

The true accounts of shootouts, train robberies and saloon gunfights like the Kinsley Train Raid of 1878 are central to Wild West lore. Hence, Kinsley, which was founded in 1873 one year after its neighbor thirty-eight miles to the west, Dodge City, has much to offer in the way of Western stories. Heroes like Andy Kingkade and villains like "Big Mike" Roarke and "Dirty Dave" Rudabaugh walked the town's streets in the 1870s and 1880s, yet still, they are only a minor part of a much more significant collage. Most Wild West tropes can be found in Kinsley's history, from biblical grasshopper plagues to piles of buffalo bones and from cowboys to unflappable saloon proprietors.

As the 1800s faded, impersonating the not-so-distant past became a treasured local pastime. Frank McGill of Lewis grew his hair halfway down his back and took up the persona of a "wild and woolly" cowboy. McGill joined the 101 Ranch Show, an extensive, pageant-like re-creation of cattle drives and confrontations with Native Americans that featured thousands of reenactors. He inspired those around him in Edward County, and soon

Harvey Jarvis (1884–1972) and Ole Olson (1888–1919) pose in their Wild West show attire, circa 1905. *Edwards County Historical Society.*

twenty-two-year-old Harvey Jarvis grew his hair just as long and set out on the Wild West show circuit.

Even though these stories of cowboys captivate us, they are the well-known tales of the West. Kinsley's hidden history is perhaps more surprising, and it is one that centers on personal and communal growth instead of gun-slinging. The early settlers of Kinsley sought to merge this independent frontier attitude and culture with the arts and humanities they brought from their homes in the East. Through this combination of Western spirit and Eastern culture, they built the community from the ground up, and by 1900, the town's population had doubled from five hundred in the 1880s to more than one thousand in 1900. Behind the wooden façades of their storefronts, this small town once described as "wild and woolly" collectively wrote poetry, busily studied Shakespeare and performed operas together. They fostered a vibrant epicenter of cultural activity fit for a city many times its size.

As more buildings appeared in town, so did the number of cultural events increase; entrepreneurs and investors prioritized performance venues to house these community gatherings, like Flohr's Opera House and, eventually, the Palace Theatre. Local amateur drama clubs, civic organizations and literary societies intermingled with vagabond entertainers, traveling charlatans, snake oil swindlers, hypnotists, multilingual automatons, elocutionists and frontier theater stars. Live performances were almost weekly activities.

By the 1910s, in Kinsley's golden age of entertainment, there was a published poet on every street and an aspiring actor around every corner. Local stars even went on to Hollywood and New York, while others published nationally. These artists combined their passions with enterprise, opened the first permanent outdoor theater in the state and formed one of the first destination Shakespeare festivals in the United States. By 1937, Professor Kenneth Wiggins Porter of Southwestern College (later of Vassar College) determined that Kinsley had the "greatest number of artists per acre." However, during the 1930s, traveling entertainers and live local performances were beginning to dwindle. The town was no longer serving as an incubator for Hollywood aspirants. Yet Kinsley had earned its now-forgotten title as the "Drama Capital of the West."

Chapter 1

SETTING THE STAGE IN THE EARLY YEARS

We define Kinsley's golden age of entertainment and culture to be the years 1900 to 1925. However, during the first quarter century of Kinsley's history, from 1873 to 1899, its citizens established the necessary foundations to support this prolific era.

Kinsley's earliest citizens held communal performances in an effort to transform the "Wild West" frontier. In the town's first five years, starting in 1873, these activities were often held in local churches. Before Kinsley's fourth anniversary was observed, the *Kinsley Reporter* announced the formation of a local organization for theatrics. Meanwhile, as this group organized, the Literary Society continued its activities with debates and even hosted performances by Kinsley's musical organization, the Glee Club. While these groups did not always memorialize their activities within the four corners of the paper, the participants stayed active. By the next year, a performance of Boston playwright George Melville Baker's *Among the Breakers* occurred. This play was part of a series of works previously released specifically for amateur dramatics. The group now went by the title of a Shakespeare play, the "As You Like It" Club. One of the club members was thirty-six-year-old Edward "Ed" Augustus Noble, a Western Pennsylvania transplant who relocated to Kinsley to convalesce from a persistent infirmity.

During this time, many people thought that the open air of the prairie could heal chronic and unspecified illnesses, so they packed their possessions and traveled westward. In Ed Noble's case, this widely shared belief was

Rufus Eugene Edwards (1841–1931), circa 1878. *Kinsley Public Library.*

correct. Once in Kinsley, the businessman began to flourish. He made fast friends with local merchant, banker and real estate baron Rufus Eugene Edwards (hereafter referred to as Eugene Edwards, as he was known). Soon enough, Noble joined Edwards's general store firm. After future Kinsley Mayor John "Jack" Marsh bought a stake in the company, it was incorporated as Edwards Bros., Noble, and Marsh. Because there was no public meeting hall to accommodate community events, Edwards hosted community events in the large room above the store.

Noble, in particular, understood the value of the performing arts and embraced that in his new, small community. While his business partners tirelessly expanded their financial positions in multiple industries, Noble participated as an amateur actor and became a benefactor of the community arts. Not only was the clean prairie air beneficial for his lungs, but the social ties developed from theatrical activities also deepened Noble's connection to the growing community. This was also true for many of his peers in Kinsley's various developing dramatic clubs. However, the workdays were long, and no one could dedicate full-time attention to the community-based arts endeavors. Kinsley's arts ecosystem also required pollination from the West's wandering artistic worker bees who were touring professional actors and musicians.

The problem for those desiring outside professional entertainment was that few touring professionals would get off the train in Kinsley with the idea of making a profit; the population was still fewer than five hundred. However, as Kinsley's local economy grew, so did its infrastructure to welcome performers of all types. In January 1878, Edwin DePuy and William Frater appeared in Kinsley with an ambitious business plan to improve the town's lack of public meeting spaces and opportunities for performers. After securing a loan from Eugene Edwards and his brother, the county's namesake, William Chalmers Edwards, the duo began creating one of the most significant structures in the Arkansas River Valley, dubbed the "Gem of the Valley" or "Gem Hall" for short. This two-story building housed agricultural "implements" for sale on the first floor, and DePuy and Frater designed an all-purpose community meeting place on the second floor.

For Ed Noble, his fellow amateur actors and his fellow transplants who were accustomed to the vibrant social and established entertainment scene of Pennsylvania, the existence of Gem Hall meant more than local pride; it reinforced a feeling of culture and connection to a greater society. So when DePuy and Frater successfully booked the Louie Lord Company to theatrically inaugurate their all-purpose community room, locals were thrilled.

Louie Lord was *the* performer on the Kansas frontier with a national reputation. Her roles ranged from light melodrama to Shakespeare, including Lady Macbeth and Desdemona. Lord, her husband and their company began touring the country in 1869 and performed everywhere from New York to New Orleans and countless small to mid-sized towns throughout the Midwest. However, in Kansas, Louie Lord found her strongest following. In preparation for her visit, the May 18, 1878 edition of the *Kinsley Graphic* (hereafter referred to as the *Graphic*) opined that she had "few superiors on the American stage to-day." While the newspapers failed to record all the repertoire performed during her week's residency, she enacted Mark Twain's three-act comedy, *Lemons* (what exactly this play is remains unclear, as current Twain scholarship has no record of it) at the conclusion of her residency at Gem Hall. Lord performed each weeknight during her stay, with some nights being "crowded to its utmost capacity." Nevertheless, Louie Lord was the exception, not the rule. Most touring performers that visited Gem Hall during this era were vagabond artists, traveling comics and even the occasional hypnotist or occultist.

Not all of Kinsley's performances were indoor shows in the new community hall. For the Fourth of July 1878, citizens assembled a massive celebration that took place in a pavilion in front of the Kinsley Hotel. It included contributions from various parts of Kinsley's cultural community; literary readings were presented along with multiple performances by the Kinsley Cornet Band and the Glee Club. When the day-long music and speaking events started to wind down, it was time for baseball, "races and other sports." The organizers even included a "Grand Balloon Ascension" to enhance the celebration. With most cultural events occurring outdoors, by 9:00 p.m. that evening, the revelers returned to Gem Hall for more music and a "Grand Ball."

In the decade to come, the 1880s, homegrown events continued at a similar rate, but big-name performances like Lord were not easy to secure. While some found this lack of professional artistic attention bothersome, like a writer did in a November 1894 edition of the *Graphic* who complained that traveling troupes had ignored Kinsley because of the "number of our inhabitants," others took it as a challenge to assemble the best homegrown talent possible. After assuming the mantle of editor of the *Graphic* in September 1881, Colonel Charles Sellers immediately began publicly pressuring the drama club to reassemble after nearly a year of inactivity. Colonel Sellers secured the Arkansas Valley Editorial Association annual meeting in town to promote Kinsley as *the* preeminent place for business. The centerpiece, outside of the extravagant banquet, was the dramatic performance of *Everybody's Friend*, which received critical praise from the *Larned Optic*, the *Newton Kansan*, the *Great Bend Register* and the *Lyons Democrat*. Colonel Sellers was successful, and Kinsley's reputation, not only for culture but also for hospitality, began to form.

THE *B-B-BLIZZARD*, CULTURAL ENRICHMENT AND HOSPITALITY, 1886

Less than five years later, Kinsley had an even more high-profile opportunity to entertain and display its enriched culture. In January 1886, a once-in-a-generation blizzard struck the region. With ten-foot snowdrifts and impassable tracks, Kinsley became the western terminus of the railroad line for a week. Packed so densely, the snow rendered train plows almost useless. Railroad administrators brought in all available men to shovel, including clerks and baggage men from every depot along the line. About six hundred men were in the force, which worked westward, while a contingent of three of four hundred worked to the east.

Passengers on trains that had made it to Kinsley were stranded in town. They slept in their Pullman cars, and the Santa Fe Company fed them at the Depot Hotel free of charge. However, according to the editor of the *Kinsley Mercury* (hereafter referred to as the *Mercury*), those snowbound people were unhappy to say the least; on January 16, he wrote that "it is safe to say…there has been more useless profanity indulged in than ever before since the founding of the town." The influx of profanity aside, the stranded train completely interrupted life in Kinsley. Businesses closed on Thursday night, January 7, and the public schools were not open until the next Tuesday, January 12, because it was impossible for some teachers to get into town.

The blizzard's repercussions continued for another week. On January 20, an Atchison, Topeka and Santa Fe westbound passenger train became snowbound in Kinsley. It was followed by a second train, a special excursion carrying vacationers from Massachusetts to California. Both trains could go no farther. With 270 passengers stranded in town, Kinsley relied on its already-established reputation for entertainment and hospitality.

Some of the passengers passed their time by writing a newspaper called the *B-B-Blizzard*, which the *Graphic* published on January 23. It contained humor, puns about the snow, a list of passengers and even poetry. One article complimented the citizens of Kinsley, calling it a "thriving young city" with "enterprising citizens." The entertainments held at Flohr's Opera House, consisting of both literary and musical activities, impressed their "involuntary guests."

During these snowbound diversions, organizers like Elizabeth "Lizzie" Sellers Edwards, daughter of Colonel Sellers and wife to Eugene Edwards, filled the evening with vocal performances and witty speeches by townspeople and passengers. Like her father, Lizzie was an especially dedicated entertainer and deeply enjoyed the arts. She was determined to make the unexpected stay not only enjoyable but also impressive. After all, the guests were from Massachusetts and other states in the East, and Kinsley had much to prove: it was not a backward and primitive location but rather civilized and cultured. The Kinsley Ladies, with Lizzie Edwards in a lead role, provided a sumptuous banquet, much like her father did years earlier. Then, Kinsley's string band played for dancing "until the wee small hours"; afterward, the "excursionists returned to the palace cars and the citizens retired to their houses."

Elizabeth "Lizzie" Sellers Edwards, circa 1878. *Kinsley Public Library*.

Lizzie Edwards felt vindicated. In her correspondences with her cousin in Philadelphia, she spoke glowingly about entertainment for the stranded passengers. She proved that Kansans were as cultured as her relatives in the East. It was a defining moment she later reflected on in letters to her family. And Lizzie was not the only one to return to this historic moment in retrospect; 130 years later, in February 2016, the *Washington Post* reintroduced this historical curiosity to the nation in a series by its "Capital Weather Gang." The newspaper noted that Kinsley provided the stranded passengers "all the comforts of home." Lizzie and her fellow hostesses would have been shocked to learn

that their hospitality was remembered more than a century later. When the passengers departed in January 1886, few could have imagined that eight years earlier, during another snowfall, the same town hosted deadly desperados instead of stranded wealthy vacationers.

The Depot Hotel, circa 1880s. *Edwards County Historical Society*.

LOCAL CLUBS AND CIVIC GROUPS, 1889

Another community leader who led events for the excursionists and Kinsley residents alike was the Congregational Church's pastor, Reverend Samuel Edwin Busser, who was now into his third year at Kinsley. Born in York, Pennsylvania, Busser was highly educated; he attended Gettysburg College and Yale Divinity School in the early 1870s. His affinity for literature fit in perfectly in Kinsley. During the snowbound days, he read poetry from Longfellow, gave benedictions and provided spiritual guidance. After the snowbound trains could finally pull away, Busser began to prepare original poetry for the Edwards County Literary Society's meeting. Not only did the Society share its original poems and essays, but it also had music interspersed with quartets, duets and solos.

As a community leader, Busser guided both religious and literary studies. However, he was but one among many who took it upon themselves to start clubs rooted in the arts and humanities. A popular topic throughout the 1880s and 1890s in the United States was the English language's most widely read playwright, William Shakespeare. Localities around the country seized the opportunity to connect Shakespeare with local civic clubs. Cora Gilbert Lewis and her husband, James "Jim" Lewis Jr., could not have missed several advertisements and notices in the local papers on the logistics of constructing these social and educational clubs. Not long after these announcements appeared in the paper, Edwards County had its very own club led by Cora Lewis.

Edwards, Noble, and Marsh General Store, circa 1887. *Edwards County Historical Society.*

Lizzie Edwards persuaded her husband, Eugene, to leave his bustling general store, Edwards, Noble, and Marsh, to attend Cora Lewis's Shakespeare Club meetings with her. Lizzie must have been proud of her success in securing her husband to attend a literary gathering, as he was often preoccupied with trade. The Edwards family sat at the center of the recent 1887 boom and substantially benefited from the influx of people. Meanwhile, Lizzie's father, Colonel Sellers, had just overseen Kinsley's local government as a mayor during two years of a booming economy. With literature, arts, culture and a bustling economy, things were looking up in Kinsley.

The Wild West Persists, 1894

The Lewis family took over the publishing of the *Graphic* in 1894. One of the first major stories they covered soon came under the headline "Our Sorrow." Much like the desperados who crept into Kinsley more than fifteen years earlier, two ruffians dreaming of Wild West adventure rode horses into town; they tied them in a corral behind a local store. The leader of this pair was Russell Carl Arnold, an unprosecuted horse thief who began his life of crime at the age of twelve, and he brought along a crony, William Harvey, whom he easily talked into the scheme. It had been five years since Arnold had run away from home, stealing along the way, and since then, he had gotten his hands on books that glorified pillaging and adventure; as he later recalled (printed in the *Mercury* on January 16, 1896), "the reading of cheap novels was responsible" for his troubles. Literature was a source of inspiration—benevolent in most cases, but this time, criminal.

The pair of Arnold and Harvey lurked around Kinsley until they identified a likely target with the most money. At the same time, Mayor John "Jack" Marsh left his store, Marsh and Bidwell Mercantile, at 213 East Sixth Street after a long day's work. Mayor Marsh was now firmly into his second decade as a successful businessman; after selling his shares in Edwards, Noble, and Marsh, he now had his own business. He also was a man who loved his wife, Susie Bidwell Marsh, and his nine-year-old daughter, Mabel. Perhaps he was thinking of them as he locked the door at 9:30 p.m. on Monday, October 22. Marsh took a few steps, and then Arnold and Harvey demanded that he throw up his hands and hand over his money. The scene was not unlike the many "cheap novels" Arnold claimed to have influenced him; it was a wide, dusty street with dimly lit, wooden façade buildings flanking them

In 1894, Russell Carl Arnold was convicted of murdering Mayor John Marsh. Image from 1901. *Kansas State Historical Society.*

on either side. Yet in this story, he was the one with the revolver. Marsh, at first thinking it was a joke, tried to wrestle the guns from the youths, but Arnold had committed to his adventure. He fired and they fled, continuing the crime spree in the town of Dighton.

Again, Kinsley was thrown into an uproar. Nearby friends who heard the shots rushed Marsh home, where he died the next day. A manhunt began across the state, and in due time, both teenage bandits were convicted of murder and sentenced to death. However, because of a moratorium on the death penalty, they evaded the gallows. Eventually, after serving fifteen years at the state penitentiary, Arnold's skill with literature (he published a book from prison titled *The Kansas Inferno*) and clever Shakespeare quoting allowed him to woo Governor Edward Hoch into pardoning him despite years of protestation from Kinsley residents. To add insult to injury, Arnold went on to commit more heinous crimes after his pardon.

Marsh's death was a major blow for Kinsley in many ways. He was a beloved merchant, friend and father, but he was also the town's mayor. How the bandits murdered him in the street also recalled an earlier era of horse thieves and train robberies, and it was deeply unsettling. It brought into question the civic and cultural development that Kinsley's citizens worked so hard to achieve. Reverend Busser, who had since been called to serve as a bishop for Western Kansas, returned for Jack Marsh's funeral. In a characteristically eloquent eulogy, printed in full in the *Graphic*, Busser honored Marsh's commitment to the community:

> *He was ever an enthusiast for Western Kansas, and often said he couldn't find a better place than right here in Kinsley. He never lost hope that these sun-kissed prairies would yet become the garden of the state, and that here would swarm a people noted for intelligence, wealth, and social influence. It is such men that develop a new country. It is such men that strengthen our credit abroad. It is such men that make Western Kansas attractive to the people of the east, and such a man was John F Marsh.*

The tragedy loomed large over the remainder of the year, but Kinsley rallied for more art, literature, live performances and increased social connections in the years to come. Many of its citizens turned to poetry, an art form that permitted them to express their joys and sorrows and to share them locally and afar.

Chapter 2

"PEGASUS WALKS UNNOTICED"

When the Atchison, Topeka and Santa Fe Railroad laid the track through Kinsley in 1873, it encouraged eastern settlers to carry their new lives westward faster than ever before. While some homesteaders still immigrated in wagons on the Santa Fe Trail, people with more means rode the steam train to their new futures. Settlers transferred books, livestock, pianos and everything they had in the East, making adjustments easier.

Just six months after the first people arrived from Boston, Washington, D.C., New York, Pennsylvania and Chicago, Ann Louisa (Blanchard) McGinnis, "a widow lady with pluck and public spirit," taught the first school with ten students. Besides her role as a schoolteacher, McGinnis held another important distinction in Kinsley's history: she was the publisher of the town's first newspaper, the *Kinsley Reporter*, before becoming postmistress as well. Meanwhile, another group of women organized the Congregational Church. McGinnis and her contemporaries were but the first of a cadre of women who led, inspired and created a new community. The prairie might seem lonely and desolate, but due to their resolve, it did not lack the arts and humanities.

In the two decades that followed their arrival in Kinsley, various literary societies and clubs formed and held weekly meetings and events; these clubs developed into different groups over time. However, the value of these activities always remained clear for residents. In November 1895, the editor of the *Mercury*, Fred Dumont Smith, attended a social gathering where the diverting evening activity was a poetic composition game. He later celebrated the event with a wry column boasting about local talent: "There [is] a whole gang of poets in Kinsley." Smith cheekily continued, noting that "every town, of course, has its peculiar greatness" before taking jabs at neighboring towns. He closed by invoking the ancient Greek myth of muses and the winged horse that delivered poetic inspiration, noting that in Kinsley, "Pegasus walks the street every day unnoticed or mistaken."

Fred Dumont Smith could not have realized how prophetic his playful statements ultimately turned out to be. He was elected a state senator in the coming years and wrote the first book published in Kinsley. However, Smith's literary achievements were only a small initial drop in the bucket. Many books, volumes, collections and individual poems were written in the coming years. If one is to believe the ancient Greeks, Pegasus did indeed visit Kinsley.

This literary output would not have been possible without the leadership of the women in this chapter: Cora Lewis, Nell Lewis Woods and May Williams Ward. These three writers inspired, encouraged and nurtured at least two generations of poets who called Kinsley home during the first quarter of the twentieth century and beyond.

CORA GILBERT LEWIS, THE DUCHESS

In 1983, Edwards County historian Myrtle Richardson explained the difficult task of trying to describe Cora Lewis's life (1866–1940). She imagined that it was like "trying to put all of the colors of the prism back into it, once they have escaped by way of sunlight." This is an apt and lively simile for Cora Lewis, a community leader and distinguish writer and poet. However, the role of poet was but one of her innumerable titles. She led a busy, fulfilling, remarkable and creative life where she balanced her duties as a mother, wife and active community member on the local and national stages; her story is one of persistence, grit, energy and even despair. She represents a binding link between many of Kinsley's early writers, artists and thinkers.

Through her untiring presence, Cora always persisted, from major national issues to items of personal and local significance. In one of her final pursuits, she and her husband, Jim, took on together, Cora fought back to save one mile of cottonwood trees from an influx of highway signs in the early 1930s. Early pioneers had planted the trees along the Santa Fe Trail in Kinsley, and they reminded local residents of the early days. Despite her best efforts, soon highway signs adorned the road in place of the once towering "sentinels," as she called the cottonwoods.

So, in the aftermath of her local loss, she turned to poetry to express her feelings. Her poem was then published in *Kansas Magazine* in November 1933:

SOLILOQUY OF AN ELM TREE IN NOVEMBER
The last brown leaf went silently away today.
Now bare and clean, drooping branches, naked—free—
Sentinel beside a lady's house,
Who loves trees in winter.
When others say "How bare and bleak are trees since November"
She will say, "How beautiful are all the trees—
Serene against the sky, still—so still
Like souls listening to God."
Watching beside her house always—
Making tracery of pictures on her windows
When winds stir about the place—
Speaking to her in mystic whisperings
In the silences of night,
Stars shining in my fingers
Sometimes the new moon in my hair—
Dappling her sunlit path
With shadows, as she walks
On early winter mornings.
Always watching beside her house—
To guard her sleep—my lady
Who loves trees in November.

In spite of this loss, with the help of her family, Cora saw many triumphs. When her father, Horace Gilbert, came to Kinsley in 1884, Cora had tuberculosis; the prescription was perseverance and the prairie air. As she went about her job as a teacher in her new community, she began to regain her strength. Horace was a successful lawyer in Missouri who believed in education for all of his children, including his daughter. When the family arrived in Kinsley, Cora was seventeen years old and had already taught school for three years in Missouri. Between the clean air and the daily sense of purpose she gained from teaching, their hope for the "prairie cure" was soon realized.

Cora Lewis at her home, Three Winds, circa 1912. *Edwards County Historical Society.*

And as often happened to a pretty young schoolmarm on the prairie, she immediately began a courtship. James "Jim" Milton Lewis Jr. had spent six years in the postal service in Washington, D.C., before coming to Kansas with his parents and brothers to raise registered horses and cattle. Cora and Jim were married in 1888, and he took her to live on the family's five-thousand-acre ranch east of Kinsley. For a wedding present, Horace Gilbert gave his daughter a collection of books. Cora had time to study these texts on the remote ranch while raising her three children: Lorraine, Gilbert and Kelton. Amid her duties on the ranch and with the young children, she hosted Shakespeare Club meetings.

From the beginning, Jim Lewis recognized his young wife's extraordinary talents and diverse interests; together, they forged their lifelong partnership. On the ranch, Cora raised prizewinning chickens and turkeys. Along with duties as a mother, she served with Jim on the Edwards County Fair Board and took on a role as a charter member of the local grange, a progressive farmers' organization. Even after they moved away from the ranch, Cora remained interested in agriculture. She wrote and spoke on farm issues, including uniting for efforts to improve marketing. Jim and Cora moved from the ranch in 1894 when they unexpectedly acquired the *Graphic* printing business in payment for a debt owed to Jim. The partnership they began on the ranch laid an essential foundation that went on to flourish in their new publishing world.

The young family moved into Kinsley and called their new home Three Winds in reference to their three children. The home exuded the art and culture Cora wanted to share with the community; according to the January 25, 1940 edition of the *Graphic*, she filled the home "with books and art objects, reflecting the exquisite taste and culture of Mrs. Lewis and her wide and varied interests." Furthermore, the Lewis home was well known as "a gathering place for well-known Kansas men and women."

The Lewis family's new role in the community as newspaper owners allowed Cora to share her talents with everyone. Cora began as the bookkeeper, and then she moved to writing the personals. In 1898, when Governor John Leedy asked Jim to go to Topeka as his private secretary, "Mrs. Cora G Lewis, Assistant Editor" first appeared on the *Graphic*'s masthead. She officially took over the editorial page, which was no small feat during an age when women were still persistently fighting for the right to vote. Her education, keen mind, extensive vocabulary, sense of humor, excellent diction and literary skills all served her well in that position for the next forty-two years.

With Jim and Cora at the helm, the *Graphic* won many awards, and newspapers across Kansas and the country picked up Cora's weekly editorials. She went on to serve as both the president of the Kansas Woman's Press Association and the Southwest Editorial Association. Cora gained prominence in state affairs and subsequently on the national stage as a very young woman. Through her membership in literary and arts organizations, she actively participated in and supported writers, poets, speakers, artists and musicians. This was especially true through her leadership in the Woman's Club and other social and literary clubs, like her early involvement in the Shakespeare Club in the late 1880s. Women's clubs were an essential part of nineteenth-century life; during the Civil War, they provided a way for women to support the Union's efforts. By the turn of the century, they had evolved and became a central part of the Progressive movement. In 1897, with nearly a decade of club experience behind her, Cora and her contemporaries expanded the Shakespeare Club's focus to a broader literary study. They founded the Kinsley's Woman's Club. The Kinsley Woman's Club's first meeting was devoted to Henry Wadsworth Longfellow and his poem "The Song of Hiawatha."

Cora's local work represented her forthcoming achievement on the statewide level. After being elected president of the newly founded Kinsley Woman's Club, four years later, in 1902, she was elevated to president of the Seventh District Federation of Women's Clubs. Then she served as president of the Kansas State Federation of Women's Clubs from 1903 to 1905. The Woman's Club advocated for reforms in education, library creation, temperance, child labor, juvenile justice, legal reform, environmental protection and more. These organizations helped start many initiatives, such as kindergartens and juvenile court systems. They tackled diverse issues like women's suffrage, lynching and family planning. Also, clubs allowed women, who could not vote and had little political standing at the time, to use their strength in numbers to accomplish their goals through sheer persistence.

With her signature perseverance, Cora went headfirst into the political battles she believed in. She stated that "women brought the home into politics, about the first thing to be done would be to get busy with a broom. Where politics touch human life, a woman should be fearless in taking part." She never feared taking a written or spoken broom to any social issue she felt needed cleaning. In 1906, she approached the governor to stop the "leave town at sundown" orders for Kansas's Black community, to build a state reformatory for women, to improve conditions in the jails and to build hospitals for tuberculosis patients.

During her years on the ranch, Cora's talent as a speaker began early. She often spoke at grange meetings to groups of farmers and continued to be called on to speak in whatever cause and group she was involved with—and this list continually grew. During her tenure as the Democratic Committee chairwoman for the State of Kansas, she addressed the National Democratic Committee, where she was proclaimed the best female speaker in the Midwest.

Because of her speaking ability and intense interest in education, Kansas Governor Hodges appointed Cora to a committee to survey the administration of the state's education. This political appointment led to the formation of the Kansas Board of Control, making her the only woman to serve in that capacity in the United States. The board evolved into the Kansas Board of Regents in 1913, and Cora was appointed to that commission as well, serving a four-year term. Later, she also served as vice-president of the National Education Association.

Ultimately, Cora found the arts equally crucial as social issues. She regularly wrote and published essays, stories and poetry for magazines and newspapers. In 1910, Cora won first prize and $100 in the Goldsmith-Woolard Publishing contest for her prose piece "A Psalm of Fatherhood." In her essay "The Winding Trail to the Stars," published in *Kansas Magazine* in 1935, she made a nod to the Kansas state motto, *Ad Astra per Aspera* ("To the Stars through Difficulties"), in her support of the arts:

> *We need a turn in the upward trail for Kansas, that turn to be marked "toward a greater love of art." Beyond this turn, we may reach the time when the public things, churches, schools, courthouses, memorials, bridges, and college buildings, will not be built altogether on a basis of cheapness and durability. It is time to remember that the enduring things built in Kansas for the years to come should be symbols of our understanding of art and beauty.*

In what "free time" she had, Cora loved to write poetry. She showcased her love of nature in her written work. In these poems, she emphasized the beauty of the prairie in every season, although winter was her favorite. Her work appeared in an edited collection by Helen Rhoda Hoopes titled *Contemporary Kansas Poetry* in 1927. One of these poems that emphasized such themes was "And Night Came":

AND NIGHT CAME
The westward falling sun
Streamed pools of color
Along the sand;
Young slender trees fringing the water's edge
Were pipes of singing winds.
Wings fluttered to high nests
Stars came out.

Tall waving grasses,
Green in the late sunlight,
Lost color and became form,
And songs of unseen things
Were heard in blue dust.
Then came a Presence all about me—
The Silence became God;
A night was born.

When Kelton, Cora's third child, was born on the ranch in 1893, the editor of the *Mercury* irreverently joked, "There is no immediate danger of the Lewis family becoming extinct in this part of Kansas." Though not immediate, danger came for Jim and Cora, and the birth announcement, in retrospect, seems prophetically cruel. Kelton graduated from Kinsley High School and earned a law degree from the University of Kansas in 1914. Two years later, he returned home to Kinsley to plan his legal career; on December 12, Kelton was not feeling well and excused himself to lie down before dinner. His father found him unresponsive, apparently having accidentally overdosed on the narcotics he had taken to alleviate his headache.

Before Jim and Cora could fully deal with the anguish of losing a child, a global tragedy threatened to arrive on their doorstep. The United States declared war on Germany on April 6, 1917, and entered World War I. At the time, Jim and Cora's eldest son, Gilbert, a practicing attorney in Pittsburg, Kansas, enlisted in the army and reported for duty at Fort Riley. Lieutenant Lewis soon shipped out to France. In the fall of 1918, the army deployed Gilbert to fight in the final drive of the war at the Second Battle of the Argonne. Gilbert had routinely cabled his parents after a battle to say that he was all right. When a cable didn't come, Cora's intuition told her that he had been killed. On November 11, she quietly stood on the porch of Three Winds. Cora wept as she waved to the joyful schoolchildren parading by celebrating Armistice Day. The War Department did not send official word of his death until early in December, confirming that, indeed, on November 2, during the last week of the war, Gilbert Lewis was killed in action. The community named Kinsley's American Legion Post in honor of Gilbert. Years later, Cora published the poem "In My Garden" in the *Contemporary Kansas Poetry* collection:

I had a garden,
And three lovely children;
Death walked in my garden,
Only one child was left.

To cope, Cora persisted with war relief efforts. During World War I, Cora donated her services to the nation in war work. She was appointed speaker in the Liberty Loan Drives by U.S. Secretary of Treasury William McAdoo (through the connections of Jouett Shouse, Cora's friend and Kinsley resident who served as the assistant secretary). She tirelessly traveled the Midwest by train, speaking along the way. After the powers signed the treaty, Cora spent six months with Anne Morgan, a philanthropist and daughter of banker J.P. Morgan, working with Chicago's Hull House in New York City. Along with Morgan and her team, Cora welcomed Kansas soldiers home and visited them in hospitals. She first headed up the Kansas Committee for Devastated France in 1921. Again, Cora's tireless efforts and exceptional work led to Morgan appointing her to head the entire southwestern United States region in that effort.

Back in Kinsley, there was still much to be done. Cora spent the rest of her life illuminating social needs and supporting literature and the arts. She was a member of the Kansas Poetry Society and the Kansas Authors Club and served on the Kansas Murals Commission. Cora Lewis became a patron of a new poetry magazine, *The Harp*, published by *Tiller and Toiler* in Larned, Kansas. May Williams Ward, the editor, was another Edwards County poet who was an up-and-coming leader in the poetry renaissance in Kansas.

The list of Cora's accomplishments far exceeds the space available to chronicle them. Her two grandchildren and other community members began calling her "the Duchess" near the end of her life because "they recognized her as royalty, or at least nobility." Then, one month before Cora died on January 18, 1940, Myrtle Richardson wrote the following:

> *Her ability to persevere, to smile through her tears, and to stick to what she knows to be fair and right, has endeared her to those of all ages who have had the opportunity to know her. Kansas newspaper circles will know no equal to our lady of the press, though it go on for centuries.*

In Cora's obituary, Leslie Wallace, publisher of the *Larned Tiller and Toiler* and *The Harp*, wrote:

> *In her death, Kansas loses an outstanding citizen, whose life and work have made an indelible impression upon her time, whose buoyant and courageous spirit has been an inspiration since pioneer days.*

NELL LEWIS WOODS, KINSLEY'S POET LAUREATE

Jim and Cora Lewis utilized the editorial page of the *Graphic* to advocate for many local issues throughout their long tenure as editors, not least of which was the formation of a public library. Kinsley's first library had been opened by the Christian Endeavor Society of the Congregational Church in 1885. Anyone in the county could join this "club" library. In years to follow, the various women's clubs all contributed to providing the library for the citizens. The ladies' clubs even ran it for a time from the back of the millinery shop on Main Street. In 1900, the Kinsley Woman's Club formed an auxiliary group to support the library. A young lady, Nell Lewis (1889–1959), began raising funds for the library even before she graduated from Kinsley High School.

Within three years, Nell joined the Woman's Club, which continued relentlessly pursuing the public library goal. The undertaking was not for the faint of heart, but Nell Lewis Woods and her compatriots could never be described that way. Finally, after more than forty years of advocacy, the proponents for a public library achieved their victory. The *Graphic* announced on April 5, 1926, that "the burden of carrying the library will be undertaken by all the people instead of the members of the Women's Clubs who have given so generously of time and money in the past" when a one mil tax levy passed. The support did not wane after this victory. Nell served on the Kinsley Library Board for the next twenty years. She, Cora Lewis and many other supporters celebrated the exciting day when the city and the Woman's Club Library became one with a mock wedding ceremony.

Cora Lewis (no relation to Nell) and the Woman's Club nourished Nell Lewis Woods's development into one of Kinsley's most celebrated literary figures. Nell's early life, however, was shaped by their father's untimely death and by her mother, Maggie, rising to the hardship of raising two children alone on the prairie. Nell was born on June 12, 1889, in Kinsley, the daughter of pioneers Diah and Maggie Miller Lewis. Her parents had arrived in Kinsley as young people more than a decade earlier. Maggie, when she suddenly became a single mother in 1892, supported and educated Nell and her elder brother Bert and provided the family an

Oil portrait of Nell Lewis Woods by Ben Ely Jr., circa 1930. *Courtesy of Rex Woods III.*

income through sewing. Nell memorialized her mother's adjustment to life on the Kansas prairie in her poem "Trailing Arbutus," which appeared alongside Cora Lewis's work in the 1929 *Contemporary Kansas Poetry*. Line four is engraved on Maggie's tombstone:

TRAILING ARBUTUS
From fruitful hills, a timid girl she came
To prairie lands that never knew a tree;
Exchanged her colored woods, her happy friends
For long, gray miles, and grim monotony;
For dim-eyed settlers always talking rain;
So hungry for her beauty-dripping land,
A hatred for the prairie filled her heart,
It spoke no language she could understand.

Year followed year; the prairie land is home,
A woman now, the lonely little lass!
Who loves the special secrets of the plains—
The brushes in the kinky buff'lo grass,
The clownish tumbleweed, the pink wild rose
(More lovely for its saucy little sharps!).
The far mirage, the strange black art it knows—
The wind-song in the cottonwood's high harps!
And yet, there comes a moment every spring—
A homesick urging all her being fills;
While here, March winds shout by with slap and sting
Arbutus peeps on Pennsylvania hills.

Nell became Mrs. Rex Woods in 1908 at the age of nineteen. On March 27, 1908, the *Mercury* described her as one of "Kinsley's most brilliant girls, universally popular, associated with the best social activities, noted for her cleverness and wit." This same year, she published her first poem in the *Bohemian Magazine*. The short toast she penned was a foretaste of the witty poems and philosophies that later made her well known in Kansas and beyond:

Drink to me only with thine eyes
And I will pledge with mine;
For I see a germ within the cup
And do not wish for wine.

The following year, after the *Kansas Magazine* published Nell's poem "The Old Sod House," Nell's literary path opened up before her. Rex and Nell moved into a new home at 604 Seventh Street to make room for their only child, Rex Junior, born on September 19, 1912. To amuse her son, Nell turned her creativity to writing nursery jingles. Thirty of these simple rhymes were published in the *Kansas City Star* in 1914, and her regular publications continued over the next few years. The following was published on June 23, 1918:

A Dog's Nose
Of all the animals that marched
And boarded Noah's Ark—
The dog came last, because, you see,
He had to stop to bark!

There wasn't room for any more
Of him to get inside—
So his poor nose stuck out the door—
And never since has dried—

Because the rains and ocean spray
Beat on his nose, I'm told,
And so unto this very day
His nose is wet and cold!

Also around this time, Nell began writing a weekly column for the *Mercury*. Titled "Down Our Way," the column consisted of short paragraphs filled with homely philosophy, sometimes sharp but always witty comments on what she saw around her, like this one from December 19 of the same year:

> *It is really better to wrap up the piece of cake in a bit of oiled paper out of a cracker box when you send it to neighbor; you will then be sure you won't be minus a napkin.*

Next, Nell started writing a new column titled "Squints" for the *Hutchinson Gazette*. Again, she wrote on folksy topics, but unlike the "Down Our Way" paragraphs, each "Squint" column centered primarily on one story and philosophy. The following, which appeared on September 7, 1919, is an excerpt from a column discussing the experience of the Chautauqua (educational and religious traveling entertainers and speakers):

> *Just before the big Chautauqua tent goes up, word is sent far and wide in grasshopperdom and chigger monarchy, and these little devils get to the grounds before anybody else; nobody objects to their coming to the grounds if they would just stay there, but that isn't the chigger and grasshopper plan.*

"Squints" led to a new column, "Over the Back Fence," which ran in the *Kansas City Star*. This column boosted her name recognition. But she always remained humble and helpful to other poets. Like her fellow members of the poetry circle in Kinsley, Nell frequently shared her poetry with others, and they shared theirs with her. For example, in the early 1920s, she and Kinsley's theatrical director, Charlie Edwards, exchanged poetry and left comments on one another's writing. Charlie referenced Nell's name and her comic feedback in a postscript he sent to the *Star*'s poetry editor while trying to get his own work published, as her work was well known from Kinsley to Kansas City and beyond.

Over the next seven years, nearly two hundred columns of Nell's philosophies, including seventy-five poems, were published and syndicated in several hundred newspapers from coast to coast. In 1929, Gorham Press of Boston published her collected works in an edition titled *Over the Back Fence*. The following poem from that book is an example of her wit:

Sam Slick was the town catch;
All the girls threw themselves at his head,
And he was so smooth
That more than one girl
Thought herself engaged to him.
However, Sam wasn't really definite about the engagement—
He just let each girl think she was the chosen one.
But he never passed out any diamonds.
He went by the directions that come with washing powder—
"Squeeze, but do not wring."

In December 1929, Nell won a prize for "There Will Be No Quarrel" as the best pictorial poem in the *Troubadour Magazine*, a poetry magazine published in California. In presenting the award, the committee wrote, "Nell Lewis Woods' poem was held to present a perfect mosaic of poignant pictures relating to a past sordid family life, and another offsetting picture of a new life. For pure picture power, this poem was held to surpass all others":

THERE WILL BE NO QUARREL
There'll be no quarrel about the gate-legged table;
You girls can have it. Please don't stare at me—
I realize its beauty and its value,
But then I know too well its history.

And in my little home's new, laughing freshness,
I do not want one thing that tells of tears—
So many symbols mark the gate-legged table!—
Conclusive picture-writing of the years;

Refinishing would not erase the memory,
Nor plane away for me that shadowed square:

The blemish from the big cough syrup bottle.—
That cough that stalks our family everywhere.

That oval marks the tidy where the lamp stood,
The round one where the sewing basket sat—
She'd sew at night, and out of almost nothing
Just odds and ends, contrive a little hat.

This knob that shows a special polished smoothness
Is where the baby found a perfect hold
To draw himself erect, see-saw, get balanced,
Than take those first small, prideful steps so bold!

A bowl that always held some grass or blossom
Made that white stain; poor dear, who loved a rose—
Yet dandelions had a cheerful color:
A flower was a flower, goodness knows!

She's bowed her lonely head here, waiting, waiting
So tense with harking as the night grew late—
He'd gone to town—she knew the weary answer.
Yet Kansas was a prohibition state.

Resurfacing would never change the substance;
Its sad patina is engraved to stay.
To me it seems a record of old sorrows.—
I want my little home things fresh and gay.

Along with Cora Lewis, Nell also became a patron of *The Harp* poetry magazine, and her poems were published in it along with Cora's. "Portrait of a Plush-trimmed Lady" has merit as a poem and contributes to the social history of "wild and woolly" Kansas in the 1880s. The following appeared in *The Harp*'s January 1929 edition:

PORTRAIT OF A PLUSH-TRIMMED LADY
Although the only woman in Hometown
Who openly followed the scarlet profession
Lived entirely without feminine companionship,
Nevertheless, death found her with women friends to spare.

Living, she was shunned more pointedly than lepers in Bible times,
For all her plumes and velvets,
Women sneered as they passed her on the street,
And men sheepishly looked the other way.

One day she died.
Mrs. Lipp, a Christian body, called several women and said
That after all, Kittie was only a poor, misguided human soul,
And that some of them ought to go
And help straighten up her rooms.

Every woman manfully answered that call;
They had a wonderful time,
Taking turns trying on Kittie's hats,
There were three with willow plumes!

Nell remained active in the local Woman's Club the rest of her life, having published extensively and serving as the Literature and Library Extension Chair of the Seventh District. She died shortly after her seventieth birthday on June 27, 1959, and is buried at Hillside Cemetery with this simple inscription: "Wife of Rex."

MAY WILLIAMS WARD, THE PRAIRIE POET

Mary Esma Williams (1882–1975) was born in Holden, Missouri; despite her given name being Mary, she was always called May. The eldest child of George and Sara Williams, May came from a family connected to Kansas's earliest days; her maternal grandfather, Captain Reuben Smith, was a Civil War veteran who served in Kansas's first legislature. When May was six, the Williams family moved over the Missouri border to Osawatomie, Kansas, where her grandfather lived.

May spent her formative years on a farm immersed in the outdoors. Her love for nature was so profound that she penned her first poem at age nine. After graduating from Osawatomie High School in 1898, she entered the University of Kansas. The small-town girl loved college life, a place that further fueled her passion for books, art and music.

When she was a senior, May met Merle Ward. After she graduated in 1905 with a degree in mathematics, she taught school for a year in her

May Williams Ward, portrait by Winfred Durstine, circa 1910. *Edwards County Historical Society.*

hometown; not long after, she and Merle were married in January 1907. The wedding took place in a little stone church that the infamous John Brown had helped build. She wrote about her wedding, "There was a light flurry of snow to frost the happy evening like a wedding cake." The couple's life followed the path of the grain elevator business that Merle was involved in. Their journey took them to various places, starting from Lamar, Colorado, and then to Spearville, Kansas (1911); back to Pueblo and Lamar in Colorado (1917); and finally to Montezuma, Kansas (1920).

May began her lifelong association with women's groups in Lamar, where she joined the Round Table Women's Club and the Ladies Social Circle of the Presbyterian Church. During these early years, May started submitting her poems for publication. *LIFE* magazine paid her five dollars for her poem "Youth Wants Summer."

Also, she was encouraged to enter the poem "Night in a Prairie Town" in a poetry contest sponsored by the Colorado Federation of Women's Clubs, where she won second prize. It later appeared in *LIFE* magazine on February 17, 1921. That same year, Merle went into the grain business for himself, and the Wards moved to Belpre, where he owned and ran the elevator. Belpre is fifteen miles east of Kinsley and on the eastern edge of Edwards County. Belpre means "beautiful meadow." May flourished there among the prairie people, who inspired her poetry. By 1922, May's poems were appearing in many magazines, as well as the *Kansas City Star* and *Topeka Capital Journal*. Within five years, she wrote more than three hundred poems and was published in thirty-five magazines.

In June 1925, May was invited to attend the prestigious McDowell Art Colony in Petersburgh, New Hampshire. This experience was a crucial moment in her career, as she spent one month there with twenty-five others involved in the arts, including notable writers such as Edwin Robinson, Stephen Vincent Benet and Sara Teasdale. Through this experience, May made significant contacts with more magazine editors, further establishing her career and reputation as a poet. Famed Kansan William Allen White, a well-known newspaper editor and author, sang her praises, which she would later include in her 1960 volume of personal reflections on her life and poetry titled *No Two Years Alike*. White stated:

> *May Williams Ward, is a Kansas poet but is more than that. She contributes to the most important magazines of verse and is easily the champion poet of Kansas. Her verse is beautiful, poignant, and understanding. She excels because she is of the prairie. She makes music out of it. Her books are the most ambitious and probably the most important coming out of Kansas just now, and will have a real ace in the poetic output of America. Mrs. Ward is one of the reasons why Kansas is proud.*

May became the unpaid editor of the bimonthly poetry magazine *The Harp* in 1925. She featured and discovered poetry from all over Kansas and the country through its pages. The *Graphic* published her poem "The Sky" on January 12, 1928:

THE SKY
Once I lived in the city,
I loved the hurry of feet,
The hours so crowded with work and sun,
The kaleidoscope of the street.

Once I lived in the mountains,
Once I lived by the sea;
The hills I loved for their steadfast peace—
The sea because it was free.

But now I live on the golden plain—
Nobody else near by…
And oh, I love it the best of all—
For I love and live with the sky.

How can I tell its beauty?
Which of its woods is best?
It makes me small as a pigmy—
It swells the heart in my breast.

By day 'tis a painted pageant.
God sketches its mighty bowl
With themes in cloud and in color
To match ever tint of the soul.

At night I gaze up in the zenith,
Far as the eye can see,
Space...and stars...and silence
Types of Infinity.

In 1931, hardship was widespread. Influenza incapacitated May for six months, and she had to give up the editorship. Even more consequentially, the Great Depression brought an end to *The Harp*. Yet in later years, May reflected on the experience, "perhaps the most rewarding activity I ever had aside from my poem-writing and selling."

May was the third Kansan elected to the Poetry Society of America, and following this distinction, she gathered her poems together and published *Seesaw*, her first book of poetry. It was followed by *In Double Rhythm* in 1933. This book, produced by hand, contained thirty poems and her original block prints.

May and Merle left Belpre in 1933 when he inherited a family hotel in Wellington, Kansas. May continued to write award-winning verse, while publishing in the *New York Times* and penning two more books of poetry: *From Christmas-Time to April* (1938) and *Wheatlands* (1954). Her poetry was also included in anthologies and textbooks. May enjoyed memberships in the Kansas Poets Society and Kansas Authors Club, serving on their committees and, at times, as an officer. She wrote book reviews, several skits for the Federation of Women's Clubs and articles on Kansas topics. Educators widely used her book *Approach to Social Studies through Choral Readings* (1945). May continued participating in local literary clubs and spoke in person and on the radio across the United States to Federated Women's Clubs, university groups, teachers and other writers' guilds.

Aloysius Sullivan, president of the Poetry Society of America, wrote about May, which Irene Hancock-Suran quoted in her 1951 master's thesis: "May Williams Ward's poetry portrays the wide horizons of the prairie, the strange loneliness and heartbreak that went with the life of the pioneer, as well as modern aspects and people of the modern wheatland and country." May's poetry reflected her life, times and experiences in

Edwards County and also resonated with her readers. May died on June 27, 1975, leaving a legacy of more than two thousand poems, seven books and a literary career that lasted fifty years.

Pegasus Noted

Many throughout the region recognized Kinsley after the successes of Cora Lewis, Nell Woods and May Williams Ward. Pegasus no longer roamed the streets "unnoticed," as Fred Dumont Smith mused late in the nineteenth century. The clubs, organizations, personal connections and collective publishing victories inspired others throughout Edwards County and beyond. In an anthology prepared for *Kansas Magazine* in 1937, Southwestern College Professor Kenneth Porter noted that "the Arkansas Valley ranks as the Fertile Crescent of Kansas poetry." The *Hutchinson News-Herald* reported on October 10, 1937, that of the fifteen poets selected statewide for publication that year, fourteen of them came from the Kinsley area, which in the reporter's opinion earned Kinsley the title of "Athens of the Arkansas Valley." Through the work of these writers, eleven of whom are included here, it is clear that poetry was a personal outlet and a collective pastime. Today, for the Kinsley community, this work remains a cherished part of its heritage.

Chapter 3

"THE VALLEY OF VERSE" AND KINSLEY'S PIONEER POETS

Cora Lewis, Nell Woods and May Williams Ward were the nucleus of Kinsley's much larger poetry circle—their backgrounds, intellect, creativity and genuine friendship united this group. The poets of Kinsley around the turn of the twentieth century were composed of two generations. The first was the group of pioneers born before or during the Civil War who had immigrated from the East—from Maine, Michigan, New York and New Jersey. The next cohort of poets was made of first-generation Kansans and others born in the 1880s and 1890s, the Gilded Age.

Here we examine the lives and a brief sample of the poetry of four of the pioneer generation: Chauncey Wells, Ida Bostwick, Alice Erwin and Ila Taylor. These four poets published their work in local papers to various degrees. Their poetry focused on their homes back east, their generation's challenges and Kansas's natural beauty.

The women in this cohort were all highly active members of the women's clubs and organizations. Like the groups managed by Cora Lewis, these organizations focused on literature, the arts and education. Ida, Alice and Ila shared their literary work with the community during public gatherings.

In December 1909, Kinsley's golden age of the arts was in full swing with weekly club meetings or performances. A Shakespearean star, Gilmor Brown, had just visited the town, and the arts crowd was abuzz. Kinsley actor and director Charlie Edwards hosted events at Trail's End, the Edwards mansion, where nearly all the poets would gather together. In one example, 125 guests attended a Christmas gathering. Following this whirlwind of arts and social activities, Cora, Ida, Alice and Ila attended an annual New Year's Day reception, welcoming the decade of 1910. It was one of many gatherings where original literary work took center stage. This poetic celebration was memorialized in the columns of the paper, leaving a record of their achievements for their descendants. This chapter examines the poets from the pioneer generation that assembled for these events.

CHAUNCEY WELLS, THE FRONTIER STORYTELLER

Chauncey Wells (1825–1909) was born the year workers completed the Erie Canal, which allowed commerce to move more easily across the state of New York. He grew up on a farm near Erieville, just thirty-five miles south of the canal.

After serving as a teacher in a nearby village schools, Chauncey continued farming. Then he married Julia Richardson in 1851, and they had two sons, Willis and Edward. When Julia died in 1880, Chauncey remarried and by 1895, he and his second wife, his brother and their families had moved to Kinsley to farm and raise Thoroughbred racing horses.

Most of the Wells family's land was in Kiowa County, just south of Edwards County. In 1900, it produced more than two thousand bushels of wheat. Additionally, one of Kansas's first sorghum sugar factories was

Horseracing in Kinsley, circa 1905. *Edwards County Historical Society.*

built on site, so the farm became known as the "Sugar Factory." Despite the name, sugar was not the primary product, as the Wells family were successful dairy farmers who raised various crops.

Very active in progressive political affairs, Chauncey ran as a state senatorial candidate on the Populist Party ticket, which was primarily composed of Western farmers. He enjoyed publishing his views and literary works in the local papers. Chauncey channeled his experiences with ranching, farming and racing into poems, which received publication. A descriptive storyteller who infused this talent into his poetry, Chauncey wrote about his horses and racing, the Fitzsimmons-Corbett boxing match, patriotism and everyday happenings in Kinsley. The following poem, which appeared in the *Graphic* on September 30, 1898, is but one example:

LOOKING FORWARD AT PARSONS
We took our two good racers down
At Parsons, from the train,
We let them loose upon the track
Upon that handsome plain.

Our Babies' eyes showing fiercely bright
As, eager for the fray,
She walked, with impatient step,
On Parsons' racing day.

Many fine steeds were gathered there,
Their fiery nostrils spread,
As eager as our own to race
And with as anxious tread. [...]

Now, now the pacing is called!
They wait the word to go!
Their thin light nostrils spreading wide,
And eye-balls in a glow.

The word is given! The pacers now
Are flying o'er the track,
And Looking Forward takes first purse
They could not hold him back.

And on Fredonia's lovely plain
Where thousands come to view,
He took 1st purse in the straight heat,
And won it grandly too.

Chauncey and his family moved to Wilmore, Kansas, where he died in 1909. He is buried at Aetna Cemetery in Barber County, Kansas.

IDA COX BOSTWICK, THE FRONT-PAGE POET

When Ida Cox (1855–1928) married the widower John Bostwick, she was twenty-seven and he was thirty-five years old. The couple left Illinois and came to Kinsley in 1885. They purchased four hundred acres just south of town between Coon Creek and the Arkansas River.

A steel engraving in the *1887 Atlas of Kansas* depicts an aerial view of the Bostwicks' neatly laid out farm. They raised pedigreed livestock, including Percheron draft horses, Hambletonian racehorses, Shorthorn dairy cows, sheep and pigs. John enjoyed racing his horses and served on the Edwards County Fair Board. The sod icehouse depicted in the engraving stored crystal-clear ice cut every winter from Coon Creek into blocks, eight to ten inches thick. It took six hundred tons of ice to keep their milk and perishables cold through the hot summer. The ice and their dairy cream provided much-appreciated ice cream for many church, school and civic picnics held under their grove of trees.

The highly organized farm could give one the impression that life on the prairie was safe and secure in the closing years of the nineteenth century, but that was far from the case. Sparks from AT&SF trains often ignited prairie fires, which were a constant threat to settlers. On March 24, 1890, such a fire spread south from the tracks and destroyed the Bostwicks' stables, outbuildings, farm machinery, stored grain, millet and hay at a reported loss of $7,000.

Because of unfortunate investments and threats like fires, the Bostwicks were forced to sell the ranch and move into a house at 822 Niles Avenue in Kinsley in 1899. The house was three houses south on the corner of the same block where Jim and Cora Lewis lived. For additional income, they rented rooms out of their home.

Ida actively created programs for the several clubs and organizations she was involved with through the years. She presented thoughtful papers on

Residence and stock barn of John and Ida Bostwick from the *Atlas of Kansas*, 1887.

authors, participated in literary debates and read her own and others' poetry. Besides being active in the Woman's Club, she belonged to the Fortnightly Readers Club and the George Eliot Circle of the Episcopal Church. During a "Gossip Party" hosted by the *Graphic* women, Ida revealed that her favorite fictional character was Jean Valjean in Victor Hugo's *Les Misérables*. Later, Ida joined a new group, the Commonwealth Club, an organization of both men and women who engaged in nonpartisan study of the day's social, ethical and economic questions.

The year after Ida's husband, John Bostwick, passed away, Charlie Edwards bought the *Mercury* (some argued that his father, Eugene, obtained it for him) in October 1907. Charlie hired Ida as a reporter because she had "exerted a helpful influence in the intellectual life of Kinsley." Ida edited the news of the women's clubs for many years, and Charlie pledged, "The *Mercury* will be eager to second the work of Women's clubs at all times."

As Ida continued her usual contributions to the paper, in February 1909, poems written under the mysterious pen name "Knott Edyter" began appearing in the *Mercury*. They immediately caught readers' attention in Kinsley and beyond, especially when Knott Edyter wrote a poem directed toward the Emporia, Kansas poet Walt Mason, whom William Allen White had labeled the "Poet Laureate of American Democracy." The *Mercury* had entered a statewide poetry competition, which was playing out on the front page of newspapers.

However, the secret identity of Knott Edyter helped boost intrigue in the poems. Ostensibly, this individual was "not [the] editor," but it seemed like the sort of humor that Charlie Edwards employed to hide the fact that he was placing his own poems in the paper. The actual writer remained a mystery, and Charlie loved it. He fanned the flames of curiosity in a March 1909 column and indulged in wordplay:

> *There is a good deal of curiosity in the county to know who the* Mercury *poet, Knott Edyter, is. Some fellows are saying that the editor writes the stuff which is getting considerable attention around the state. Now if the editor is not editor he doesn't know who is, but at the same time he states positively that he is not Knott Edyter and defies anyone to prove the contrary.*

Meanwhile, in this same edition, the *Mercury*'s "front page poet" wrote a poem titled "Kinsley, Kansas." This poem encourages a revitalization of the city, but rather than the real estate and business booms of the 1880s, this upswing was cultural:

> *Where the sturdy shortgrass crinkles,*
> *And the golden sunflowers bloom,*
> *There the town of Kinsley, Kansas*
> *Is developing a boom.*
>
> *Not a boom like those you've heard*
> *Of in the days of long ago,*
> *But a boomlet calm and peaceful,*
> *And yet strong enough to grow.*
>
> *For the people have decided*
> *There's a chance for Kinsley still,*
> *And that's why they're getting busy*
> *And are working with a will.*

They want another railroad,
A Knights of Pythias Hall,
And a fine new High School building
And they're working for them all.

And that's why they're going to have them
When they've carried out their plan.
Can they do it yes, indeed, sir!
That is just what Kinsley, Kan.

The enigmatic "Knott Edyter" wrote thirty-seven poems throughout 1909. Other towns and their newspaper staff attempted to copy them, but these poets did not have both the rhyme, rhythm and momentum that Kinsley's front-page poet had. Publications in Kansas City picked up the work as well. On the first of January 1910, after Ida, Ila Taylor and Charlie attended the annual Women's Club reception, their works were printed in the *Mercury*. In this edition, Charlie revealed that it was indeed Ida Bostwick who held the nom de plume "Knott Edyter." After that, Ida's work appeared infrequently, only briefly reemerging for the presidential election in 1916. However, her prolific year as the *Mercury* poet prepared her to publish her own volume of poetry, which she did in 1915 with *Some Kansas Rhymes*.

Charged with the collective energy of the literary arts in Kinsley, Ida wrote diverse poems covering many moods, including ones that were gifts for people celebrating an anniversary, birthday or some other personal event. She was an active participant in Kinsley's cultural life until her death in 1928. Ida Bostwick is buried beside her husband at Hillside Cemetery.

ALICE HUMPHREY ERWIN, THE PIONEER POET

Alice Humphrey (1859–1944) came on the train to Kinsley in 1873, during the town's founding year, when she was fourteen. Her journey to Western Kansas was not unlike many of her contemporaries, yet she differentiated herself. In the coming years, she contributed her form of poetry, raised a vibrant family and had her work published locally and nationally.

Alice was born in Maine, where her father, Nicholas Humphrey, was a sea captain. In 1864, President Lincoln appointed Captain Humphrey as consul to Port of Spain on the Trinidad Islands in the West Indies. As the captain's health deteriorated, he gave up his post. Like many others seeking better health, he signed on as part of the original Massachusetts Colony that settled in Kinsley in 1873. Captain Humphrey purchased a quarter section of land two miles north of Kinsley and broke up the soil with oxen.

The following year, Captain Humphrey's wife, Lucy, came to help build a simple clapboard house out of two-by-fours covered with heavy paper and then wallpapered. This dwelling was much better than the sod houses and was considered the best house in Kinsley at the time. Soon after, Alice and her two elder sisters, Francis and Harriet, arrived by train. More than a half-century later, Alice recounted her first impression of Kinsley:

> *I distinctly remember that morning when we stepped, from the creaking, groaning old* [train] *cars in Kinsley. It took six days to make the trip from Boston. We made our way to the roughly, constructed hotel, unplastered and dimly lighted, the odor of pan-cakes filling the air....Never shall I forget that first sunrise; not a tree or a house to obstruct the view or to prevent our seeing the first peep of old Sol as he rose, so far away, over the long stretch of prairies so new to us.*

Not long after arriving in Kinsley, Alice began participating in entertainments. She was exceptionally well known for her "elocutionary power," or her performance of the spoken word. After earning much praise from the small developing city in the newly formed Edwards County, Alice returned east to attend Lake Forest School for Girls and graduated in elocution and voice. Upon her return, she met William Dilworth Erwin at her parents' home. William was in the lumber business at Edwards and Erwin, which the indomitable Eugene Edwards partly managed. Later, he bought out Edwards's share in the company, as he had plenty of other business interests.

The Erwins had six children and lived at 416 East Seventh Street, where Alice enjoyed entertaining and recalling her days of elocutionary amusements. Her children followed in her footsteps and were actively involved in Kinsley's vibrant arts scene, each taking roles in the renowned Shakespeare festival.

Alice, a pioneer member of the Women's Club, presented an original poem at the group's annual reception on New Year's Day 1910 with her friends Charlie Edwards, Cora Lewis, Ida Bostwick and Ila Taylor listening carefully. She wove together natural imagery with visions of "Fairyland" and a renowned line from the large quantities of Shakespeare she and her friends

The Woman's Club (including Alice Erwin) at a breakfast picnic on the grounds Meadowbrook Theatre, Kansas's first open-air theater, circa 1925. *Edwards County Historical Society.*

absorbed. She included a *Merchant of Venice* line ("All that glisters is not gold") in her poem printed in the January 12, 1910 edition of the *Mercury* titled "Winter Is King":

WINTER IS KING
The cold and pitiless and dreary rain
Beating, beating with relentless sting
Sparing neither bush nor tree nor passerby
In dull monotony declares Winter is King.

What varying mood are his:
The north wind is his champion bold.
Also the light and heat of day,
The great and glorious sun tempering the cold.

What transformation hath he wrought;
Great is his might and magical his power.
For lo! The gray and barren tree
A thing of beauty is in one short hour.

These dull and desolate and dripping boughs,
Filling some hearts with gloom so sad,
Waving aloft his magic wand,
By this same king, all glistening are clad.

Plume after plume, waving in the air,
Gazing, transfixed we stand,
And then with bated breath we cry,
Ah, indeed this is fairy-land!

But even as we speak, alas,
The glittering fragments fall,
And shattered, melt and fade away,
Like pots of gold and fairy visions all.

Silent we stand and ponder long,
Upon the adage old,
Declaring unto mortal man,
That all things glittering are not gold.

And still we think and ponder,
And know beyond all gold,
Are the things that never perish,
The true heart's wealth untold.

Writing, however, would not always be easy for Alice. In the coming years, she began to lose her sight. Despite this developing blindness, a condition she would live with for forty years, Alice's resilience was evident in her longtime participation in the Congregational Church. Her faith and talents were sources of inspiration for many. On Easter Day 1944, she had the pleasure of knowing that her Easter poem appeared in a nationally known magazine, the *High Road*, and that she had received second prize for her poem "Song of the Wind" in the poetry contest conducted by the Seventh District Federation of Women's Clubs.

Alice broke her leg at the age of eighty-five and was unable to recover. She died on April 16, 1944, not long after, still believing, "I am a loyal Kansan, thankful that I left the east, with all its age and wealth and glory, to grow up in the wild free air of Kansas."

ILA CARMICHAEL TAYLOR, THE BARD OF LAFALOT

Ila Taylor (1862–1941) was born in the small village of Washington, New Jersey, amid the Civil War. The seventh of eight children spread out across twenty-three years, she was always surrounded by family growing up. For the rest of her life, there was nothing more important to her. Around the time she finished schooling at age sixteen, her brother Ed Taylor, eighteen years older than her, took his family west in search of the opportunity that eluded him. His destination was Kinsley.

The young and creative Ila chose to stay behind in New Jersey, as there was still opportunity for her at home. Soon she married Louis Hann, the First National Bank of Washington's head cashier. Her new husband wasn't just a cashier; he was also the son of the bank's founder and a local judge. Ila had married well, or so she thought. After the birth of her daughter, Louise, and her son, Augustus ("Gus" for short), in 1886 and 1888, respectively, in 1891, the Hanns' marriage collided with hardship. The tiny village erupted into scandal. Rumor persisted that Hann had thrown his wife down a flight of stairs during an altercation. The papers further noted that he had "otherwise cruelly treated her." As a result, Ila fled with her children to New York.

Seeking a divorce, Hann concocted a plan to frame Ila for infidelity, designed to grant him custody of their children. As Ila went about her daily business, her estranged husband had her "shadowed" by nefarious "private detectives" who were then to testify against her in court with maliciously fabricated lies. The September 20, 1892 edition of the *Jersey City News* sensationalized the trial with articles like "Shadows on Wedlock: More Disgusting Testimony by the Detectives in the Hann Divorce Suit." During their time on the witness stand, the "private detectives" proceeded to slander Ila's character. Ultimately, the vindictive Hann and his cronies failed, and Ila received custody of the children.

After the public divorce proceedings were covered in the smallest and largest papers, Ila penned a healing poem popular in *Munsey's Magazine*, published in February 1894. She named her verse "Morning" and lyrically described how each morning vanquishes the shadows, no matter how deep or long they may be:

MORNING
The tempest may dash on the vale and hill,
But the sunshine smiles behind it;
The caverned rock hides the mountain rill,
Yet a tiny gleam can find it.
Gladness will fall upon grief's cold breast
And soften the voice of its warning.
Over the darkness sweet hope will rest,
And after the shadows—comes morning.

As the nineteenth century faded, more adversity awaited. Ila had more shadows to conquer. First, her estranged husband died in 1897 of "softening of the brain." Later, she lost her sister in a terrible accident, and then, one year later, another brother passed away. Yet Ila remained resilient. In 1900, she lived comfortably with her two children, presumably working in an editorial capacity with some of New York's largest newspapers, as she later told her friend, onetime *Mercury* editor Charlie Edwards. In a few more years, her daughter, Louise, married and was off to make her own home.

When 1906 arrived, Ila's son, Gus, was now eighteen and interested in farming and carpentry. But to explore this, he needed a job and to escape his childhood in the bustling city. Ila, determined to create a new life for her family, seized the opportunity her brother Ed's offer presented. Mother and son stayed with their relatives on their homestead south of the Arkansas River and fell in love with the community. Then they decided to permanently leave behind New Jersey and dark reminders of the past, embracing a hopeful future in Kinsley.

As Ila settled in Kinsley, she took on a new role as the Country Woman's Club president. Ila's leadership and dedication to the community inspired the women around her, and her home became a popular locale for club members and others to visit. She often opened her bungalow to even friends of friends, which she and Gus had now whimsically and joyously dubbed "Lafalot in the Sandhills," no doubt because of her affinity for a good laugh. Neighbors from all over town regularly trekked south of Kinsley on horseback to visit her in the sandhills.

Ila dedicated her energy to showering any pessimism she found with a visit to Lafalot. It simultaneously was a place in the sandhills and a state of mind. At a Women's Club Federation meeting, Ila took to the stage. She told an assembly of people, including those featured in this chapter, a cheery story "of a tired woman" who visited a neighbor. The neighbor said, "Oh, dear, come in: my veranda hasn't been swept this morning." "Never mind," replied the other woman, "I was looking at your honeysuckles." Ila encouraged her audience "to look at our honeysuckles in Kinsley." In her mind, one could always find something beautiful if only people could slow down and look.

In 1911, after being single for nearly two decades, Ila remarried. Her last name almost remained the same, though, as the lucky man was Thompson Haun. Thompson was a Western Kansas pioneer, lawyer, cattleman and the founder of nearby Jetmore. He divorced his wife, Elizabeth, of thirty-five years to marry Ila. They lived in a house on the northern edge of Kinsley, and she continued with literary and poetic work. She also became a well-known speaker and received invitations to speak at many events, including conferences throughout the state and an annual appearance at the Edwards County Farmer's Institute.

By 1916, Ila was presiding over the Kinsley Woman's Club meetings in town as progress with women's causes, including suffrage, became more palpable. World events stretched Ila's personal resolve when her son departed for the muddied and bloodied trenches of France. He wrote home to his mother as often as he could. At times, when appropriate, his notes were published in the Kinsley papers. Captain Augustus Hann barely escaped his service on the battlefield after being gassed and suffering several broken ribs.

Perpetually seeking to find light in the dark, Ila wrote patriotic music to honor the service of the American troops who risked everything. Her sheet

The Woman's Club at the Kinsley Depot, featuring many of the poets in the chapter, circa 1910. *Edwards County Historical Society.*

music for "Our Yankees Are on Their Way Home Again" was published in April 1919 and featured a photo of Gus in uniform; it was a celebration. Storefronts throughout town proudly displayed the work of the town's first published composer. Unfortunately, the merriment was bittersweet.

Around the same time the music was published, Ila's second husband died at sixty-nine. Shortly after that, in early 1921, Ila Taylor Haun married for a third time, this time to businessman Allen Renick of Lawrence. She said farewell to her loving community and to Lafalot in the Sandhills, and the couple relocated to Ponca City, Oklahoma. Irrepressible as always, Ila found a new circle of friends in a writer's club. There she shared her poems like "Sanctuary" and "The Voice of the Pioneer Woman." But perhaps most revealing, she wrote a piece alluding to her lifelong aversion titled "Fleeting Shadows."

Ultimately, she was never afraid to do what she needed to do. In 1937, at age seventy-five, she filed for divorce against her third husband, claiming that he was habitually drunk. The divorce was granted, and the court also permitted her appeal to "restore" her first name, Ila Carmichael Taylor,

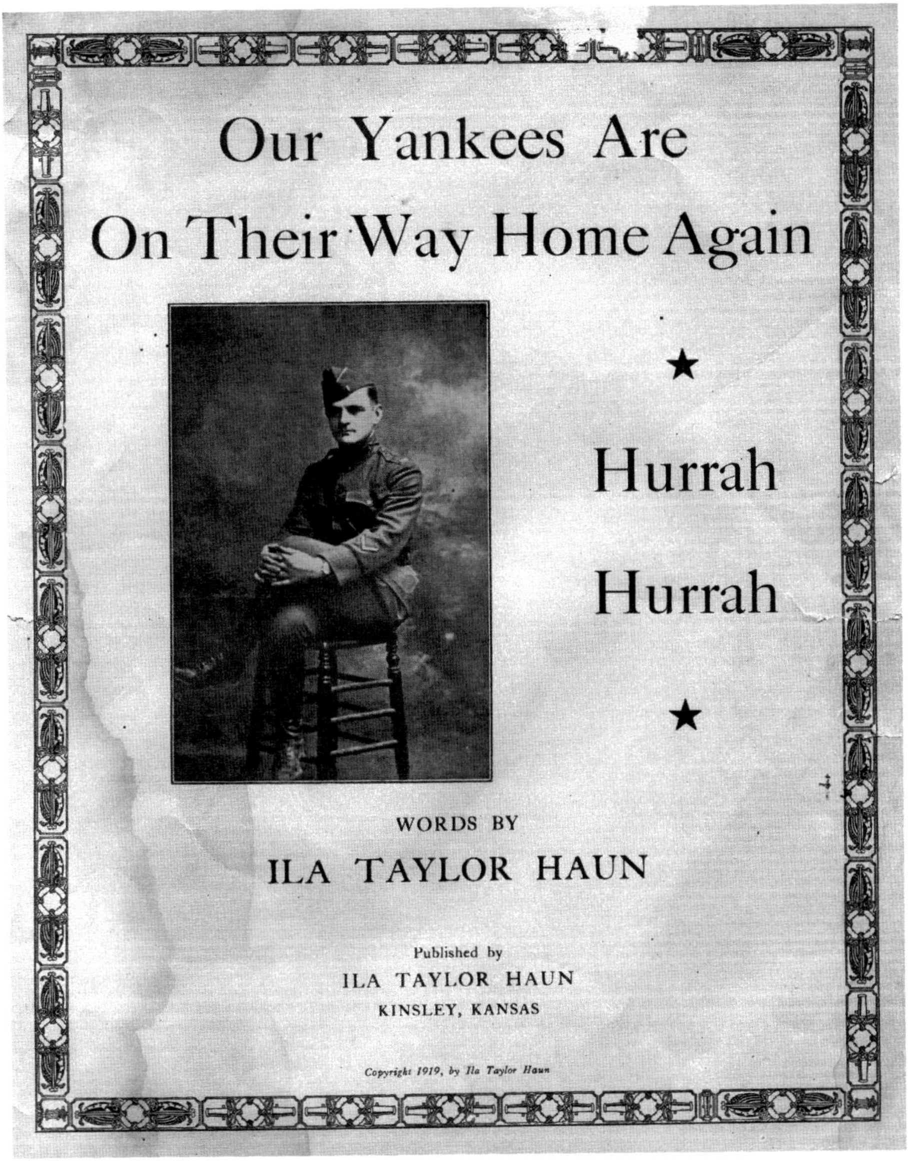

Ila Taylor's patriotic music written for her son, Gus (featured on the cover), 1919. *Edwards County Historical Society.*

discarding the remaining nomenclature of all three husbands. When she passed away four years later in 1941, she was seventy-nine and living in New Jersey, where she is buried. She was mourned by her beloved son, the veteran Captain Augustus Hann.

Chapter 4

"RETROSPECTION"

Poetry in Kinsley's Golden Age

Americans born between the 1880s and 1890s—like Kinsley poets Billy Gartner, Charlotte Moffat, Hazel Buxton and Charlie Edwards—came to age in a transformative time. Their youth was influenced by a rapidly developing sense of optimism and widespread civic patriotism. However, the horrors of World War I and the 1918 flu pandemic redefined their outlook. As such, the poets featured in this chapter depart from the pastoral ideas of the previous generation; instead, their work focuses on disillusionment, mourning losses and navigating newfound freedoms. Also, they explored the not-so-distant past and how it affected their uncertain present.

Like their elders, these four poets developed a close bond through the community's literary, civic and church life and turned these experiences into verse. Examining their lives and poetry allows one to glimpse how they enriched the cultural life of Kinsley during its golden age of the arts.

MAJOR WILHELM "BILLY" GARTNER, THE SOLDIER POET

Wilhelm "Billy" Gartner (1883–1922) lived in Kinsley for only five years but stayed connected for several more and always cherished his time in Edwards County. Billy Gartner graduated in the 1903 class from Punahou Preparatory Academy in Honolulu, Hawaii. This private, coeducational boarding school was founded in 1842 and still educates students today (President Barack Obama graduated from the academy in the class of 1979). As a senior, in the fall of 1902, Billy exhibited his poetic skills when he wrote the words for Punahou's alma mater during the football season. The students still sing it to the tune of the German folk song "O Tannenbaum":

> *Oahu-a, Oahu-a; Punahou, our Punahou;*
> *Mau a mau, O mau a mau; Punahou, our Punahou.*
> *For hundred years we've shown our light.*
> *We glory in Oahu's might.*
> *The Buff and Blue's a glorious sight,*
> *Punahou, our Punahou.*

Billy married Maude Alice Coffman and arrived in Kinsley in 1905. The family bought land south of the river, where they intended to raise mules. However, Billy soon changed his mind and started a fruit farm. They named their country home Cyraquail, and the couple soon entered Kinsley's social life, entertaining at their home.

During their five years in Kinsley, their first daughter was born, and Billy had two poems accepted by the *Kansas Magazine*, "A Pipe Dream" and "Old Flames and Cigar Smoke." In 1910, Billy decided to make another career change and entered medical school. The family moved to St. Joseph, where he studied medicine for the next four years. While studying, the Gartners kept Cyraquail and returned in the summers to check on their property and see their friends.

When Billy graduated, now Dr. Gartner, he and his family moved to Troy, Kansas, where he set up his practice. Their second daughter was born in 1916 as World War I raged in Europe. Wilhelm helped prepare by setting up Red Cross First Aid and Nurses' Training in Troy. When doctors were needed after the United States declared war on Germany on April 6, 1917, Dr. Gartner answered the call. He passed his exams and was admitted to the U.S. Army Medical Corps, receiving a commission as a lieutenant in June.

Dr. Gartner reported to Camp Funston at Fort Riley in Kansas in August 1917. He did not know that by spring, he would be at the beginning of another war when a deadly influenza pandemic, known as the Spanish flu, started at Fort Funston. The soldiers then carried the epidemic on the troop ships going to Europe, and then it spread from Europe to the rest of the world. The CDC estimates that this influenza virus was responsible for

The Arkansas River by Kinsley photographer John Cox, taken near the home of Major Dr. Garner, 1912. *Kinsley Public Library.*

50 million deaths worldwide; the United States alone lost 675,000 people to the disease.

Promoted to captain in April, Dr. Gartner arrived in France to care for the wounded and sick. He came to the aid of the wounded at the Battle of Saint-Mihiel and both Meuse-Argonne drives. In November, he went to the front in the last battle of the Argonne to retrieve the injured, above and beyond his call of duty. Due to his valor, he was severely gassed and had to be hospitalized. When Dr. Gartner, now a major, returned home, a delegation from Troy met his train and gave him a hero's welcome. He immediately resumed his practice and became the county health officer.

One of life's ironies soon manifested itself when a little insect did what the gas, bombs and influenza had been unable to. Toward the end of June 1922, Dr. Gartner was bit by a chigger on his foot. Despite treating the sore with iodine, it became infected, and blood poisoning set in. He went to the hospital, where it continued to worsen. One must remember that penicillin had not been invented at this time, and infections caused by wounds and chiggers could be deadly.

Dr. Gartner began to have bouts of delirium, which brought back all the terrors of the recent war; he imagined charging with the victorious troops at Saint-Mihiel and tried to warn others about the bloody Battle of the Argonne, which had ended years earlier. When he was not delirious, he talked to his wife about how he reconnected with his earlier life. He dreamed of writing children's stories and poems while recovering on the porch at home.

During his last fit of hallucination, the nurses tried to cool him with an alcohol bath. He drove them from the room and jumped out of the two-story window. The fall broke his arm and fractured his skull, and he died on June 30, 1922. It is uncertain whether he might have recovered from the blood poisoning, and this caused controversy over the cause of his death, whether from the fall or the blood infection. His death was ultimately ruled to be blood poisoning from an infected chigger bite.

The following poem by Major Gartner captures the essence of postwar trauma, survivor's guilt and disillusionment. It was reprinted from the *Troy Chief* in the *Mercury*, on July 6, one week after his death:

RETROSPECTION
How strange it seems that four brief years ago
With them, we heard shells whining by.
Nor dreamed that sometime we would long to go
Across the seas, where old pals lie.

We who dream dreams of Yesterday
With them, of a crusade to foreign lands,
Was it Chance who snatched their lives away.
And spread Oblivious shifting sands?

We who walked with them, where grey mist blows,
We who crouched with them, on the torn hill.
Ah Mirror of Eternity who knows
Why we are here, yet they lie cold and still?

What Destiny took those at Saint-Mihiel?
What whim of Fate, left us, still marching on?
What scheme of things, gave us another deal;
Yet let good men die, there in the Argonne?

Life reached its climax, for them alone,
With shrapnel bursting ever overhead.
How strange that we are—those come home,
Instead of sleeping with the Hosts of Dead.

The *Mercury*'s editor commented, "The many Kinsley friends of Major Billy Gartner will be glad to read his beautiful poem, but the unanswerable questions in it—must be and are unanswerable."

CHARLOTTE GRACE NILES MOFFAT, THE POET OF THE PARLOR

Charlotte Grace Niles Moffat (1884–1972) was born in Arlington, Virginia, to Frederick Alonzo Niles and Melissa Brown. Charlotte may have inherited her poetic skills from her father. During the Civil War, First Lieutenant Frederick Niles fought in Company D of the Forty-Ninth Illinois Volunteers at Shiloh, and he is credited with writing a poem reflecting on the war, titled "Daisy of the South." While Frederick published his poetry, Charlotte, one of six children, was educated in Arlington and Washington, D.C., schools.

In 1904, Charlotte married Arthur Moffat in Hyattsville, Maryland. Their first years were spent in Philadelphia, where their son, Niles Moffat, was born. Soon, Arthur and Charlotte joined family members seeking a "prairie cure" and moved to Kinsley. Charlotte immediately began to adjust to her new surroundings as Arthur began working for a prominent Kinsley lawyer. Arthur passed the bar in 1911 and became a partner in this local firm. Around the same time, Charlotte was busily writing papers and becoming enveloped with creative and literary energy in Kinsley. She joined the Woman's Club and became an active member.

Women's club events highlighted life's educational, civic and social aspects. One example was a 1914 costume party where Charlotte joined fellow poets as famous historical women. Charlotte dressed as Charlotte Corday, a French Revolution–era assassin, while Nell Woods embraced her own name in history, too, and went as Nell Gwyn (a seventeenth-century celebrity actress and mistress to King Charles II). Other active clubwomen like Alice Erwin and Ida Bostwick also the donned the attire of impressive women from history.

Charlotte remained in the women's club for the rest of her life; she even served as president in 1919 before giving birth to her second son, David, in 1920. She and Ida Bostwick gave one program together on child welfare in 1923 and remained closely associated with these issues as well. She also was a life member of the Kansas Authors Club and the Daughters of the American Revolution (DAR) and belonged to the Order of the Eastern Star.

Following a lengthy illness, Charlotte died in 1949. In 2001, Charlotte's son David collected her poetry into a volume titled *Poetry by Two Graces*; it

Sixth Street, 1911. Charlotte Moffat's husband joined the law practice on the second story of the first brick building on the left. *Courtesy of Julie Ackerman.*

is on file at the Kinsley Public Library. Her work reflects rural life during her day as well as the seasons, weather and the natural beauty of the world around her (and worlds elsewhere). She emphasized her fellow club women and the many hours they spent together at her home, in her parlor and around Kinsley. Charlotte's poem "In Memoriam" reflects on the many years they spent together at the beginning of the twentieth century, while both mourning and celebrating her members:

IN MEMORIAM
They've gone on ahead to greet the dawn;
Those brave Club Women, our Pioneers.
With steadfast faith they carried on,
Nor wasted time in needless fears.

They laid the course, we weakly falter
Along the path their feet so firmly trod.
Theirs was the faith, they raised the Alter
That led their steps at last to God.

We miss the pleasant smile, the friendly handclasp,
The encouraging word they never failed to give;
But we have their fine example still before us,
And in our work their influence will live.

HAZEL MOSHER BUXTON, THE GARDEN POET

Hazel Mosher (1891–1987) was the daughter of pioneer Kansas physician Benjamin Reynolds Mosher and his second wife, Ella. Dr. Mosher was a dedicated "buggy" doctor who went out on calls at night and in any weather. He owned and operated a drugstore on the corner of Sixth Street and Marsh Avenue in connection with his medical practice. Also a racehorse owner, Dr. Mosher, bought land just south of Kinsley, where his daughter, Hazel, helped train the horses as a girl. Consequently, Hazel became an excellent horsewoman.

In 1911, Hazel graduated with honors from Kinsley High School and attended a finishing school. Within four years, she married Albert Buxton, who had been her high school principal, science teacher and basketball coach. During their marriage, Albert had left teaching and worked as a cashier for the Farmers' State Bank in Offerle. On their wedding day, they went on separate trains only to secretly rendezvous in Newton, Kansas, where they were married before continuing to Kansas City, where Albert attended a banker's convention. The following week, they returned to Offerle to live and begin their family of two daughters, Helen and Mary.

The Buxtons lived in Hutchinson for a short time before returning to Kinsley in 1921, when Albert went to work for the Kinsley Bank. A decade later, he became the bank's second president, taking over after the death of longtime community business leader Eugene Edwards, and he was there until his death in 1937. Besides being a good wife, mother and Sunday school teacher, Hazel liked writing poetry, directing plays, painting pictures and gardening.

Over the many years, Hazel would consistently teach Sunday school at the Congregational Church. On July 22, 1922, the *Graphic* chronicled how the churches organized a Sunday school parade and picnic complete with floats and "ponies with their bright ribbons of color and bicycles with their streamers and woven wheels." Hazel Buxton's love of dramatic production and Alice Erwin's artistic ability was evident in the creation of the Congregational Church float, which took first prize for its artistic costumes and theatrical flavor. It depicted seven women of the Bible, three of whom were Kinsley poets: Hazel Buxton as the Queen of Sheba, Nell Woods as Miriam and Alice Erwin as a mourner.

Despite dust and drought, Hazel grew roses and lilacs in her beautifully kept garden at 503 Fourth Street. One longtime Kinsley resident remembers spending time with Mrs. Buxton; she found her garden quiet and peaceful.

Hazel Mosher Buxton (*center*) and her future husband Albert Buxton; actress and singer Lucile DeTar stands on the far left, circa 1910. *Edwards County Historical Society.*

Hazel invited her and a friend into her home and told them stories about the strict rules she had at finishing school. The children had fun walking around with books on their heads and mimicking the airs that Hazel described.

Hazel's love for poetry was deeply intertwined with her passion for her garden. The garden served as a muse, inspiring much of her verse. This connection between her garden, the passage of time and her poetry is captured in "Quiet Sound":

QUIET SOUND
I've learned to listen for quiet sound…
The whisper of roots in thawing ground;
Or the under beat, elusive and wary,
Of solitude that pervades the prairie…

The misty patter of shadow feet
Along a shaded country street
And the brooding silence that always follows
The swift ascent of chattering swallows…

The continual drip of the sands of time
Recording events from the world's pantomime
And through all the echo of God's pulsation
Rhythmically coursing throughout creation.

The tones that the outer ears elude
Converge to lyric interlude
Filling my heart with joy of fearing
My soul may go deaf with exquisite hearing.

Her poems were published in several poetry journals, including *Better Verse*, *Westward*, *Step Ladder*, *The Occult Digest*, *Colorado Look Out* and *Kaleidoscope*.

CHARLIE EDWARDS, THE KANSAS ROMANTIC

While subsequent chapters cover parts of Charlie Edwards's (1880–1926) extensive theater career, this section includes a brief account of his poetic experience and personal qualities.

Charlie, a Kinsley native, began his published poetry career early and was much more at home in the theater or with a pen in his hand than working in one of the many businesses owned by his father, Eugene Edwards. His inability to rise to his father's side and take over the family business remained a source of constant tension between them. Moreover, his disposition was at odds with the standard expectation of men. His written work often alluded to what many often whisper about: that he was a gay man. As such, one of Charlie's contemporaries remembered him decades later: "He was the banker's son—a sissy type fellow....I don't think he knew how to be like the other boys." Likewise, scholar Delmar Homan described Charlie as the "Kansas Romantic" in an unpublished 2004 essay, noting his lifelong "yearning for love" and a proclivity for depression.

Charlie centered the topic of naïve, true love in his earliest (extant) published work. This poem appeared in *Metropolitan Magazine*, a nationally renowned publication, titled "The Reason," in December 1900, right around his twentieth birthday, under the nom de plume "Brandon Culver." When he became the editor of the *Mercury* in 1907, he continued to print poetry and his own literary column. In 1909, Ida Bostwick's stint as Knott Edyter helped him keep the original poetry flowing throughout the year. After leaving the post in 1911 due to severe anxiety and depression, he turned to his extensive theatrical endeavors, where his focus remained for a decade, publishing poetry only intermittently.

In the 1920s, Charlie turned to poetry to battle his ongoing and persistent struggle with his mental health. He maintained poetry as his expressive personal outlet, while theater kept him occupied during the days. Always fiercely patriotic, Charlie was thrilled when the *New York Times* published his elegiac "He Sleeps His Night of Stars" in November 1921, which memorialized the many soldiers lost in the Great War, like his friend Gilbert Lewis, Cora Lewis's son. Charlie did not just publish his poetry in New York City; he also lived there on and off from 1916 through 1921. Following major performances with the Washington Square Players and other New York theatrical companies, Charlie went to the Hotel Algonquin, where he wrote poetry. He wanted to be near the epicenter of the literary and critical world, and he found that at the Algonquin Round Table. However, he did not stay long to rub elbows with America's most famous writers; Kinsley called him home.

Once he returned home, he returned to poetry. The following poem was printed in the *Kansas City Star* on March 1, 1924, two years before his death. It recounts the moment when the reader meets a deeply missed lover while emphasizing Charlie's lifelong fascination with fairies. The poem dramatically diverges from his first publication, reflecting the change in cultural values and the passage of time between 1900 and 1924:

MEETING AFTER MONTHS
And we will meet again
   And we will kiss,
And all the world's disaster
   In that bliss,
And all of ecstasy and all of tears
Will mingle with the breath of flowers fading
through the years
Since we have met; then they will blow
   *Away *   *   **
And yesterday, today, will be today!

An instant I will hold you off,
   And I'll behold
The little scars of tangling branches
   Overbold;

And then the faery rapture of our fire
Will leap to flame, as leapeth sound to lyre,
Blazing that heaven which is you and I,
Where poignant trumpets of the golden
angels cry!

In the subsequent years, Charlie had many poems published in the *Kansas City Star*, *Kansas City Times* and other Kansas papers, with some syndicated in other cities around the country. However, much of his moving poetry was never published. Fortunately, it still exists in manuscripts, capturing the essence of his personal struggles, Kinsley's progress and the nation's turbulent transition from the Gilded Age to the Roaring Twenties.

Chapter 5

From Vaudeville to Shakespeare

Theater in the Early Years

The closing decades of the nineteenth century were part of a remarkable and captivating age, especially on America's Western frontier. This was, in part, by design. The storytellers, actors and entertainers who captured America's West in real time helped to forever immortalize it. Despite popular depictions, these legends-in-the-making were more than the tales of rugged vigilantes and bandits. Those who created this mystique were the entertainers, the vagabond quacks with multilingual automatons and frontier theater personalities. They still can capture one's imagination.

Ultimately, the performing arts provide individuals and communities with diversion. For those populations trying to build a civilization from the ground up, the varied amusements did more than provide a fleeting laugh or shallow chuckle. These cultural events bound together shared values and connected settlers to their distant heritages, all while creating a new sense of identity. Some of the events, like Professor Robertson's hypnotism or Professor Norris's Dog Show, were lighter and silly, and others were proudly homemade and consequential. These amusements, which eventually blossomed into a large-scale Shakespeare festival, brought together the majority of the community in one place to share moments of levity, introspection, pride and even catharsis.

On Sunday mornings, the people of Kinsley went to different church buildings and were inspired by leaders like Reverend Samuel Busser. But when it was time to view their shared community entertainment, they all went under one roof, in a single crowded room, to share a human bond that, especially today, remains intangible.

THE LOSS OF GEM HALL, 1878–1879

When Louie Lord, actress extraordinaire, and her company stepped onto a departing train after inaugurating Gem Hall, many in Kinsley feared that it would be some time before they secured a star of her caliber again. These concerns were well placed. In August, Gem Hall's proprietors booked the Hernandez Parlor Comedy Company. The group, led by twenty-six-year-old theatrical wanderer Montie Hernandez, announced that their entertainment was a popular vaudeville act. This bill included "songs, dances, farces, etc." It guaranteed some local attendance, especially since, as the *Edwards County Leader* reminded locals on August 22, 1878, this "kind of entertainment does not often visit Kinsley."

Expectations were high for Hernandez's performance. He grew up as a member of a theatrical family and lived every moment of his life in the business. Hernandez had assisted superstar "can-can" performer Giuseppina Morlacchi in her visit to his family's theater in Sioux City, Iowa. However, all of his experience with the dancing, comedy and raucous shows of the West did not predetermine success on the stage, especially in Kansas. Hernandez's specialty in low comedy parts failed to resonate with audiences that enjoyed Louie Lord's Shakespearean and melodramatic prowess. The *Graphic* leveraged the opportunity to take a jab, a common occurrence for rival newspapers, at the *Leader*'s "kind of entertainment" that rarely visits Kinsley: "and we confidently hope visits from such said may be even more seldom." Other newspapers from settlements along the railroad that the Hernandez Company visited, like the *Arkansas Valley Democrat*, corroborated this criticism and excoriated the performance by calling it "snide," before elaborating further: "Their poor rendition of stale jokes was received with hisses and shouts of derision by the audience, and all felt that an imposition had been played upon them."

Kinsley did not hold "saloon shows" of ill repute, popular in neighboring Dodge City, in high regard. With quality touring vaudeville options still few and far between, getting close to what was known as the "legitimate theater" seemed like a distant dream for those in Kinsley desiring a connection to this form of cultural refinement. Shakespeare's plays were on the bookshelves of

An artist depiction of Gem Hall, 1878. *From the* Kinsley Graphic, *Edwards County Historical Society*.

Kinsley residents, but to the chagrin of many, with Louie Lord's single visit now a memory, the plays were not anywhere near the stage of the Gem Hall.

Kinsley's performance venue's luck would not improve. On the forcefully windy twentieth of April in 1879, a blaze broke out near the City Palace Saloon. Within seconds, nearby residents across the street heard an explosion, and before the alarm sounded, an entire building succumbed to fire. The inferno engulfed between one-half to two-thirds of Kinsley's business district: the post office, markets, drugstores, clothiers, hotels, banks, saloons and businesses of all types smoldered. Amid the coal-black scars lay the remnants of Kinsley's pride, Gem Hall.

THE CALKINS HALL YEARS, 1879–1886

Eugene Edwards, who lost several buildings in the fire with a combined value of nearly $5,000, announced plans to construct at least five stone and brick structures. One of the buildings he helped to finance was the next incarnation of a public meeting and performance location: Calkins Hall.

Almost immediately after the destruction, businessman Samuel Isaac Calkins and his son, Fredrich, who had relocated a year earlier from Brockton, Massachusetts, prioritized the construction of a "larger and more commodious" hall. Locals were delighted to learn that Calkins Hall was to surpass its predecessor in every respect. Calkins announced the building's perimeters by the end of May 1879: a "first class style" at sixty feet long by twenty-three wide and over ten-foot-high ceilings.

The Calkins family envisioned this center for performances, entertainments and meetings. This rebuilding plan emphasized the social, cultural and economic importance of this type of all-purpose meeting and performance structure. They secured the land from Eugene Edwards. Despite the great pride the press took in Gem Hall serving as the public meeting hub, the editor of the *Valley Republican* needed very little time to move on from its previous attachment. After the new venue was finished, the newspaper proclaimed, "Our new town hall has been named after the builder, Calkins. It is a relief to get rid of that old name Gem, and we are glad Mr. Calkins decided to give it his own name."

Regardless of its nomenclature, Calkins Hall served the Kinsley community for the exact purpose its designer intended. Dances and concerts appeared as the most common forms of entertainment hosted at the new hall, but the venue was a haven for a wide variety of activities. General public meetings on public welfare, Presbyterian Church services, a "mammoth" art gallery, theatrical tableaus, ice cream festivals, political conventions and even a "gambling device" all found a home in the same space.

In the early years of Calkins Hall, its proprietors did not go out of their way to contract with touring performers; nevertheless, some still appeared. Even though there was only a modest amount of money to be made for either party, some performers tried; agents occasionally disembarked the train for solo performers and wandered to the central performance venue. Full theatrical companies like Louie Lord's or Montie Hernandez's had become rare. However, the nationally known Billy Arlington secured a gig in town in early September 1879. But, again, a professional performer failed to live up to the hype. Perhaps Louie Lord had set the bar too high, or maybe Kinsley preferred the literary greats to the comic buffoons. The *Kinsley Republican* editor noted that the "advertised humorist" delivered "what he call[ed] wit" or jokes that had been "heard for a score of years."

With quality professional performers so hard to secure, the stage in Calkins Hall supported at least six community-based dramatic clubs composed of amateur performers in the early 1880s: the Gem City Dramatic Club, the Southside Dramatic Club, the Kinsley Dramatic Club, Dramatic Club No. 2, the Independent Drama Club and then the alliterative Kinsley Komedy Kompany. The *Graphic* encouraged the development of local drama and artistic performances on December 13, 1879, with the following quip: "Anything to break the monotony." While participation in the events from general townspeople was broad, the support from the local business and civic leaders was what ultimately made the difference.

Kinsley's most influential firm, Edwards, Noble, and Marsh, supported these local amateur performances in various ways. While finances naturally helped, perhaps most influential, the company's leaders became actively involved. An early event organized by Lizzie Sellers Edwards and the Congregational Society involved her father and current newspaper editor, Colonel Sellers, on stage and a new star acting alongside favorite Ed Noble. This breakout star was Lizzie and Eugene's two-year-old son, Charlie Edwards. Noble played "Old America," and little Charlie played "Young America." Immediately, Charlie's theatrical prowess was spotted. Colonel Sellers wrote at the top of his *Graphic* editorial on March 29, 1883 (albeit, as the grandfather, he was biased), "Young America showed his sand last Friday night," an idiom that roughly means "showed what he's made of." Kinsley's earliest stages were theatrical incubators for the next generation.

The year 1884 brought a surprising development to town in the form of a craze that was sweeping the nation: roller skating. By March, the incredible amount of skating from the first three months of the year ruined the floor in Calkins Hall. Kinsley was without a performing venue for the first time in years. Twenty-three-year-old George Mumper, who had recently moved from Pennsylvania, came up with a solution by December; he began constructing a facility to be used as a livery stable on floor one and skating and public performance on floor two. As Mumper hurriedly completed this structure, Lizzie Edwards and the Ladies Society organized an amateur theatrical on a stage constructed in the Congregational Church. Lizzie and the other organizers had originally planned to host the production at an outdoor ice skating rink, as skating was still tremendously in vogue; however, a bitter cold snap prevented it. Ed Noble portrayed the "Ice King" in the production, perhaps as real-life foreshadowing for the Blizzard of 1886, which was to come in a little more than a year.

By early 1885, the damaged Calkins Hall was now serving as a grocery store, so Mumper's barn, lecture hall and skating rink combination were the only places for public performances. However, placing large groups of people over a barn with horses and their associated odors was not a winning business model. Mumper's rink closed as the skating fad ended; in fact, all of Kinsley's rinks closed in a few years. George Mumper went on to be a successful shoe manufacturer, his performance hall/stable idea notwithstanding. This absence allowed an entrepreneur to come along and provide a venue specifically designed for performance. Local businessman Gustav Flohr seized the opportunity.

FLOHR'S OPERA HOUSE AND TOURING ENTERTAINERS, 1885–1903

Flohr was a fifty-year-old German immigrant who fought for the Grand Army of the Republic in the Civil War. He opened various businesses after moving to Kinsley in the 1870s with his wife and four daughters. By the mid-1880s, he had earned enough funds to invest in creating Kinsley's only "Opera House." The German American had already built brick buildings in town, and his word was sterling. In early 1885, the press kicked up the excitement buzzing around town. The *Mercury*'s editor, Sam Vandivert, echoed a familiar refrain: "Kinsley has far more home dramatic talent than is usual in towns of this size." Therefore, he suggested, "when our new hall is completed let us furnish our people with entertainment" instead of "cheap" shows that travel. Lastly, the editor suggested the money made with the home dramatic performances be appropriated for a public library building. The idea connected theatrical activities to the town's public expansion, and consequently, Flohr's Opera House remained the heart of this civic-artistic formula for nearly three decades. A new era had begun.

Gustav Flohr's choice of name for his new performing venue was neither accidental nor arbitrary. This decision represented mainstream practice for signaling the level of cultural and moral activity that was to occur within its four walls. Communities throughout Kansas and the nation christened their community performance spaces "opera houses" to indicate that their space represented a place of refinement, not a place associated with low-brow shows of disrepute, even though very little opera occurred within their walls.

With the opera house now complete, Kinsley could finally realize its collective aspirations of a permanent drama club. There were two amateur performances in the fall of 1885: *Rebecca's Triumph* and *Queen Esther*. However, amateurs vanished from the bills after the Blizzard of 1886. During this significant moment, the opera house served as a community hub, one that Kinsley's residents proudly exhibited to their snowbound guests. Gustav Flohr welcomed at least six traveling companies into his new opera house the following year, including the triumphant return of Kansas's favorite performer, Louie Lord.

For children in Kinsley, like the young aspiring actor (and future poet) Charlie Edwards, who was now at an age where he could begin to absorb the theatrical performances he saw, 1887 was a tantalizing year, even after Louie Lord finished her show. The town was in a boom year, and Charlie's grandfather Colonel Sellers sat at the helm as Kinsley's mayor. Economic accelerants fueled cultural activities, optimism pervaded every household and yesteryear's financial and agricultural difficulties faded. Gustav Flohr took the opportunity to lease the opera house to a theater manager to bring in "the best show talent on the road." This strategy gave the community plenty of theater and social opportunities. Unlike years past, traveling shows and amateur performances now appeared regularly.

Community members established merit judging committees after disastrous performances like Montie Hernandez and Billy Arlington to critique traveling entertainers. After all, local theater lovers should only be exposed to the very best. Other performing companies were less concerned with the performance quality than with the believability of the products they sold during their entertainment. In October 1891, one of Healy and Bigelow's Kickapoo Indian Medicine Companies set up their tents, tepees and stage in Kinsley's city limits. There they gave free performances nightly for two weeks, designed to sell as much of their cure-all quackery as possible. Around 1890, Healy and Bigelow claimed to have contracted nearly eight hundred Native American performers for their traveling shows. They placed them in the roles (usually as villainous antagonists and only occasionally as benevolent healers) to peddle the most "authentic" natural remedies, which included their signature "snake oil" called Sagwa.

With historical hindsight at our disposal, it seems patently obvious that the company's founders, Healy and Bigelow, were capitalistic white men seeking to exploit Native American performers in every way for their own financial gain while scamming anyone they could in the process. Healy and Bigelow's Kickapoo companies saw incredible popularity and success despite these unethical methods. Their business model relied on the same gullibility and performative techniques of the mountebank performers of Europe who peddled medicine in the prior century. Healy and Bigelow's primary addition involved exploiting nostalgia for the age of "frontier America," days that were rapidly fading with the advent of Edison's light bulb and the "civilizing" of the Wild West.

Placing nostalgia aside for a brief moment, early in 1889, Lizzie Edwards and her peers at the Ladies Society schemed a wholesome production designed to break up a monotonous and not-so-prosperous winter. The local 1887 boom was definitively over, and the town was rapidly losing population, causing ripple effects in all sectors, especially in entertainment. The ideal time for a community-based theatrical to reenergize everyone's spirit had arrived. Lizzie and the other club members identified the perfect play and jumped on a theatrical bandwagon titled *The Deestrick Skule of Fifty Years Ago*. A state officer of the Woman's Christian Temperance Union (WCTU), Mary Jaquith of Topeka, wrote her own form of what had toured around the country for decades—shows that embraced an earlier time, long-gone halcyon days—called "old folks concerts." Jaquith's version transformed what was traditionally a music concert into community-based theater, best characterized as an entertainment sensation. Due to its clear objectives, *Deestrick Skule*'s structure harkened toward a future era of community theatricals. The play was unabashedly designed for large casts of amateurs with the flexibility to adapt to the locality where the play was being produced. Nostalgia was making another comeback.

Playwright Mary Jaquith created a premise for this play rather than a plot: local community members of all ages portray American schoolchildren from the late 1830s. Throughout the play, a schoolmaster aurally quizzes his students, and they comically answer the question incorrectly; he moves on to the next question without acknowledging the absurd errors. This wholesome formula appealed to audiences. The play emphasized nostalgic elements showcasing remarkable improvement in American education in a half-century. While Jaquith playfully lampooned America's early educational system to appeal to the country, the script contains unambiguous state-specific references. One student character dubbed "Jay Hawker" reads aloud his "Composition on Kansas," with references best appreciated by audiences within the state. Also, *Deestrick Skule* was customizable; it was local entertainment *by*, *for* and *of* a local community. With its author fully immersed in issues that appealed to women in Kansas and nationwide, the play exploded in popularity.

Charlie and Marion Edwards in Elizabethan costume as children, circa 1887. *Kinsley Public Library*.

At least thirty productions enlivened audiences in thirty different Kansas towns and cities before Kinsley rehearsed it in February 1889. When the Congregational Church mounted the production, it achieved Jaquith's stated goals in the script and created a veritable "who's who" of Kinsley. With the cast they assembled, the group ensured solid attendance and fundraising figures. After the cast had concluded their preparations, opening night at Flohr's Opera House arrived. As the audience filed in, almost everyone noticed a family member (or two) and many friends on stage. Young Charlie Edwards and his sister, Marion, certainly met this description; they did not sit with family, as every family member was on stage. Twenty-eight people participated, seventeen men and eleven women, only limited by the stage size at the opera house.

As the stage crew opened the curtain, Schoolmaster Higginbotham stood proudly in front of his class of young scholars. An overjoyed Charlie saw his grandfather Colonel Sellers, the town's mayor, take on this leading role. With another glance, he and Marion saw their father, the venerable capitalist and rancher Eugene Edwards, playing a child named Hezekiah Butterworth. As if having two family members on stage were not exciting enough, the children also proudly looked on to see their mother, Lizzie, gleefully taking on the part of Prudence Ann Plunkett. Meanwhile, others like Jack Marsh and Ed Noble took similarly entertaining roles.

Charlie watched his beloved grandfather hopelessly try to solicit correct answers from the incompetent adults as children. The *Graphic* noted that the large crowd appreciated the performance and these varied jokes, especially the youth, who were stunned at the "funny sight" of seeing Kinsley's most "staid and dignified middle aged citizens" try to recall grammatical, historical and geographic facts through quasi-improvisatory theater. Through Kinsley's production of *Deestrick Skule of Fifty Years Ago*, Charlie Edwards absorbed a formative community-based theater experience. He joined a large and admiring crowd of his fellow townspeople assembled at Flohr's Opera House to view a multigenerational production featuring his parents and grandfather. With them, he laughed and exclaimed pride in his community and family.

Theater was so beloved by Kinsley's population that its citizens jumped at the chance to have another show composed of home talent. This desire presented opportunities for those willing to cheat, steal and make a buck at others' expense. After all, charlatans came in many shapes and sizes, and they did not always sell snake oil. One such unexpected deception came in the form of a touring community-based theatrical director, the twenty-one-year-old Charles B. Kendall. This supposed director from New York got off the train peddling a community performance of Longfellow's poem "Evangeline," in which a lead actor (Kendall) read a poem, while a tableau took place behind him on stage. He brought press clippings that proved his show was a success in other states, a business model that capitalized on the many communities that yearned for local performance but lacked the people to carry it out. The only problem was that the "Kendall" referred to in the clippings was not the Charles Kendall in Kinsley contracted to direct the latest home-talent show, but rather his "brother" (they were not biological brothers) or former business partner, Preston Kendall. This other Kendall was a reputable performer who originated the business model, and at some point, the two had a falling out and began performing separately.

With little talent outside quackery, Charles Kendall blundered his way through producing "Evangeline," which included fifty locals at Flohr's Opera House. He cast seventeen-year-old Charlie Edwards in the lead male role. Charlie immediately noticed that the organizer of the production was ill-equipped for the job. When Kendall failed to deliver Edwards's cue line, the young actor was incensed. Ever since he was little, with his performance at age two, Charlie had envisioned a career in the theater. Charles Kendall made a mockery of the careful work one needed to do in order to cultivate that work; some said he could scarcely provide the proper enunciation of the words he read.

Fred Dumont Smith, the editor of the *Mercury*, whose wife played the titular character, Evangeline, corroborated Charlie's feelings on the matter, stating that Kendall had "an unfortunate disposition for such efforts." Editor Smith continued in this January 1898 review, making the matter of charlatan theater directors quite clear: "He is rude and ill-bred and came very near having a riot on his hands several times." While Kendall failed to pass the critics test, Kinsley still fared rather well. In several other towns that Kendall visited in Kansas, he pitched the idea and collected the funds from trusting local groups that wanted a play that was professionally produced. After he had all the money, he skipped town without organizing the play. In July 1898, the *Ottawa Daily Republican* issued this warning to the state: "He may come here." Kendall evaded the authorities and went to Nebraska, where he continued his charlatan theater directing for more than a decade before serving a prison sentence in New Mexico.

Meanwhile, the struggle for quality "legitimate theater" remained a problem in town. The Shakespeare Club was now meeting at the home of Cora Lewis, and many prominent townspeople joined the proceedings, but alas, Shakespeare was not playing at Flohr's Opera House. To the chagrin of the club members, instead, a more universally celebrated entertainment appeared: Professor Cozy Norris (whose real name was Clarence Cozad) brought his "Dog and Pony show" to Kinsley. The entertainment was not complex; the "Professor" had his small dogs perform feats that amused the audience. Nevertheless, novel or not, Norris was on to something. In 1891, at the time of this performance in Kinsley, he was well into the ninth year of his touring show. By the end of the century, the group had grown into a nationally known circus, Norris & Rowe's. A steady stream of circuses visited Kinsley in the years to follow, including the Campbell Brothers from Fairbury, Nebraska, in August 1898.

Those wishing for a performance of a sophisticated variety got their wish when a performance by elocutionist Mary Calhoun Dixon was announced. As an elocutionist, the nineteenth-century equivalent of a glorified public speaker, Dixon performed classic literature through perfect articulation, enunciation and projection. Most notably, she was an exception to many rules. In the public eye, she was a single working mother, an almost unheard-of situation. She embodied a future few men could envision; she balanced

The Campbell Brothers Circus parades through Kinsley, August 16, 1898. *Edwards County Historical Society.*

her motherhood with a full-time professional job, all while inspiring many in the towns in which she performed. Not since the boom year in 1887, when Louie Lord made a reappearance, had Kinsley hosted a performer with such grace and sophistication. Dixon enthralled the audience with a bit of Shakespeare and other classics. Unfortunately for literary enthusiasts, the audience for Dixon's elocutionary readings was smaller than the audience for Professor Norris's Dog and Pony Show or Campbell Brothers Circus. The editor of the *Graphic* did not hold in his displeasure: "If we continue to fill the house for a dog show and give a wide berth to those of [Dixon's] class, we shall find in time that it is only those of the former class that will gravitate towards us."

The dramatic performances that were to come alleviated the concern that all entertainment was only of the circus variety. In 1895, Charlie Edwards began a lifelong directing career at the age of fourteen. Based on the many community-based performance experiences he had as a young child, he founded the Young Peoples' Dramatic Club. With this new group, Charlie assembled an elaborate example of "parlor theater," a form of entertainment that occurred in homes throughout the nineteenth century. The event marked the first time the young man directed in Kinsley. His productions became a staple in the community for the next three decades, but first he had to further his education. Edwards left the following year to attend Dillenbeck's School of Oratory in Kansas City. Meanwhile, amateur performances continued, and literary clubs developed more programming.

When Charlie returned to Kinsley in the subsequent years, full of ideas and dreams and holding a degree in elocution, he found a small, thriving city teeming with business, agriculture and the arts. His dreams of attending Yale did not pan out; instead, he made his own remarkable future in Kinsley.

VISITING SHAKESPEAREAN STARS, 1904–1911

No other playwright appears on Kinsley's playbills at the frequency of William Shakespeare. From 1904 to 1916, Shakespeare's plays were a constant companion at club meetings. Early in this period, the plays were fully staged for the first time at the opera house.

The enthusiasm for Shakespeare that began all those years earlier at Cora Lewis's home with the Shakespeare Club continued into the early years of the twentieth century. Now rebranded the Fortnightly Club, the group's leaders were Lizzie Edwards as president and her son, Charlie, now back home from his undergraduate education in Kansas City, as vice-president. One of their earliest events was a large Shakespeare birthday party performance. Charlie volunteered to provide the theatrical portion of this reception, while others recruited involvement from local literary clubs in Dodge City and Larned. These members also wrote papers on Shakespeare and brought them to the event to present. Topics for the evening included "Shakespeare, the Man," while others were more regionally and specific and appealing, like Cora Lewis's "The Shakespeare Clubs of Kansas" and "The Effect of Shakespeare Study on the World-Famous Characters of Dodge." That night of the performance, Charlie Edwards inaugurated Kinsley's era of Shakespeare with Hamlet's famous "To Be or Not to Be" speech, captivating his audiences. None of the attendees could predict that it was the beginning decade of Shakespearean performances that led to regional renown.

The following year, the Shakespeare event proved to be such a success that the Fortnightly Club organized a similar event, complete with guests attending in Elizabethan costumes. A banquet and theatrical activities took place at the new home of Eugene and Lizzie Edwards, with their son serving as Master of Ceremonies. The family dubbed this newly christened Edwardian mansion "Trail's End." While gathering together for fun, fellowship and food was undeniably a large part of the appeal, Shakespeare was seriously studied by the group's members. The group explored Shakespeare in many contexts, from the plays in Japanese translation to special guest lectures on the lesser-known plays. For example, Daniel Baugher, Kinsley's longtime school superintendent, came to the club to present research on the fifteenth-century English civil war, known as the Wars of the Roses, which are covered in Shakespeare's history plays. Kinsley's Shakespeare studies were intensive scholarly pursuits that established a sturdy foundation for the years to come.

With interest as high as it had ever been for Shakespeare's works, a professional touring actor and his company arrived in town at just the right time—in fact, just three days before Shakespeare's birthday—with a complete Shakespearean production. Flohr's Opera House hosted an entire Shakespeare play performed by Sanford Dodge, a forty-year-old Minnesota native who had just embarked on a theatrical tour through Western Kansas. The April 13, 1906 edition of the *Graphic* correctly noted that he was the first to visit "the smaller-sized cities." It could have been perceived as risky, but many towns in the region were starved for "legitimate drama," especially Kinsley. Thus, Dodge's *Julius Caesar*, the first Shakespeare play ever performed in full in Kinsley, was celebrated. The *Graphic* wrote, "Kinsley is very fortunate to have so good a company present a Shakespearian play, and our people feel personally grateful to Mr. Flohr for the privilege of seeing it." The review closed with the hopes of seeing more of Mr. Dodge.

However, three days later, another entertainment appeared on the opera house floorboards. In direct contrast to the praise of *Julius Caesar*, it was met with harsh condemnation from the local critics. This company, called the Ward Minstrels (minstrelsy was a widespread form of low comedy built on racist stereotypes of African Americans and involved the application of burnt cork to create blackface), received a tepid response at first; "part of the entertainment was fair," the *Graphic* wrote. Next, however, the critic explicitly denounced the performance, not because of the explicit racism, as this was the era's cultural norm, but instead because of its sexually suggestive content. The paper explained the outrage:

> *A would-be woman impersonator with a limited amount of clothing and less sense, did a stunt that was the most indescribably stupid and vulgar performance that the writer has ever seen upon the stage.* [He] *could neither sing nor dance, but his offensive contortions captured a certain element and they writhed with joy. Their applause was deafening, and a second and third presentation hardly seemed to satisfy.*

The editorial went on to explain that the new management of the opera house wants "good entertainments" such as Shakespeare, but some "companies take advantage of his kindness of heart." They closed with a final stinging rebuke: "One can stand poor acting, mediocre singing, awkward dancing, but when the limit of decency is passed it is time to express public disapproval." While some in Kinsley clearly loved a bit of low and inappropriate comedy, the press wanted to keep the town safely focused on legitimate theater, like Shakespeare. With his plays, they could build civic pride, organize community events and even create scholarly work, but through minstrelsy, the *Graphic* argued, all they would find would be depravity.

A similar situation repeated itself in 1907 when Sanford Dodge reappeared in town to take on Shakespeare's infamous "starcross'd" lovers in *Romeo and Juliet*. As it was one of the "highest class" events in the season, everyone was encouraged to attend. This season, however, Kinsley was also focused on a gradually increasing number of homemade dramatic events. By 1907, the tradition of local performance in town was over three decades old, but until this moment, the events were spaced out so that it was common for the most performances per year to be no more than two to three. This was

Kinsley Big Brothers Club at Trail's End, 1910. Eugene Edwards is at far left; Charlie Edwards and Lorin Raker are seated, left pillar; Tom Mairs is seated, center. *Edwards County Historical Society.*

now beginning to change due to a mix of educational performances, which started at the school and then moved to the opera house and community-based shows.

Sanford Dodge gave his farewells after providing an opera house performance and a parlor performance at Trail's End of *Romeo and Juliet*, sponsored by Charlie Edwards. The ongoing theatrical enthusiasm had already encouraged Charlie to round up a few locals for entertainment at the annual Arts and Crafts show. Charlie chose a two-act comedy, *Sweet Hearts*, featuring Nell Lewis (Woods) and a newcomer to Kinsley, sixteen-year-old Lorin Raker. The performance was well received and established as a starting point for the young performers.

Theatrical performances became more challenging for Kinsley's increasingly busy impresario to manage after he bought the *Mercury* and became its managing editor in October 1907. Charlie Edwards now held this influential local post with his new title, just like his grandfather Colonel Sellers, who managed the *Graphic* in the early 1880s. Occasionally, he found time to organize an event like the variety show "Café Vaudeville" in December. Although his primary responsibility now was writing, he still found a way to blend his passion for theater into his business responsibilities at the newspaper; he became a small-town theater critic.

One of editor Edwards's earliest theater critiques was of *The Castaway*, directed by a local husband-and-wife duo who directed shows for communities from Larned to Dodge City and Garden City. While Charlie utilized some space in the column for the entire cast and the directors, he mainly focused on Lorin Raker. As someone who had gone to school to learn the art of theater and as one who had learned of its triumphs and difficulties, Charlie shared his analysis of the up-and-coming local star:

> *Among the amateurs, pleasing as they all were, Lorin Raker's work stood out as that of a beginner with real temperament....But we believe that should be start on the Long Road, we, his neighbors, ought to lend a hand by giving him all the judicious encouragement we can....Lorin, if you do go in, win—and may God bless you!*

Charlie's public encouragements printed in the *Mercury* on December 20, 1907 were essential. Lorin continued to perform in local plays for the next several years, even directing one at the high school before receiving a professional gig in Wichita—and that was just the beginning of a remarkable career.

Chester Mairs ('13) and Lorin Raker ('11) in a theatrical production, circa 1911. *Edwards County Historical Society.*

While editing kept Charlie Edwards busy, he still found himself participating in local theater. He could not resist the opportunity to play a role in the Kinsley production of Gilbert and Sullivan comic opera *H.M.S. Pinafore*. The cast included a chorus of forty voices and a ten-piece orchestra. Both newspapers, Charlie's *Mercury* and Jim and Cora Lewis's *Graphic*, excitedly and proudly drummed up interest in the production: "Every man in Edwards county is going to see *Pinafore*, and so are his sisters and his cousins and his aunts." Charlie decided to prepare the audience by breaking down the plot on the front page of the *Mercury* to "increase their enjoyment of the work when presented."

Amid the buzz about the locally produced comic opera for the opera house, the *Mercury* editorial team also included a look back at another event that occurred in the very same structure twenty-two years earlier, the infamous Blizzard of '86. The column chronicled that "the story of their stay has become like unto a folk tale in this neighborhood." Meanwhile, another column commented on Governor Hoch's response to his pardon of convicted murderers who killed Mayor Jack Marsh, Carl Arnold and William Harvey. Bandits, blizzards and buffalo had been replaced with the cultural offerings of operas and Shakespeare, but the Wild West heritage was

Sailors from the 1908 production of Gilbert and Sullivan's *H.M.S. Pinafore*, January 1908. *Kinsley Public Library*.

still very much a part of Kinsley's collective memory. While Charlie, club women and the literary societies focused on Shakespeare, others, like Frank McGill and Harvey Jarvis, celebrated this aspect with participation in both traveling and local Wild West–themed theatrical productions.

More Shakespeare was to come, however, and it was always celebrated by the press; after all, Charlie Edwards led the *Mercury*, and Cora and Jim Lewis commanded the presses at the *Graphic*. Promoting literary works was only natural in Kinsley at this time. Announcements soon came for "Shakespearean Event of the Season"; a company of Shakespeareans led by experienced actress May Stewart was preparing for its Kinsley debut. A rising star in her company had worked his way from the smallest parts in Sir Ben Greet's touring outdoor Shakespeare companies to midsized parts in touring throughout the Midwest and Canada. His name was George Gilmor

Brown (he went by his middle name, Gilmor), and he played the male lead, Orlando, in Shakespeare's *As You Like It*. This comedy marked the third full Shakespeare play to be performed in Kinsley, and it received rave reviews.

The rest of the year in entertainment failed to live up to this standard. A play came to town called *The Devil*, which the Kinsley's theatrical critic excoriated in his November 25, 1908 review: "When we are more civilized than at present such dramatic spectacles will not be put before [our young people]." Even a silly musical comedy could not appease the difficult editorial board, likely composed just of Charlie. He remarked on a traveling musical company:

> *Musical comedy is not a high form of theatrical entertainment. Its only excuse for being is its possibility of dragging enough laughs out of the human animal to put his overworked faculties in the proper state of relaxation for a good night's sleep.*

With poorly acted and vulgar theatrical offerings appearing on the bills, the next Shakespeare opportunity seemed all the more desirable.

Until Shakespeare again appeared, there was no lack of local dramatic entertainment. In October, locals performed a short play titled *The Goal*, followed by an original play written in Kansas titled *Snap Shots*, which featured many locals, including Charlie Edwards, Lorin Raker, Nell Lewis Woods and Ida Bostwick, among many others. Charlie also took over the direction of the high school plays and produced Gilbert's *Pygmalion and Galatea*, featuring Lorin Raker and up-and-coming actress Lucile DeTar in the lead roles. Another local opera, *The Chimes of Normandy*, followed it only weeks later. When the summer "off-season" ended, there was only a brief wait before Gilmor Brown returned to Kinsley with the next Shakespeare offering.

This time, Gilmor led his own company. His production of *The Merchant of Venice* received so many accolades that Charlie Edwards wrote him afterward asking for an encore performance. Gilmor, who was on a Kansas tour, accepted the offer and turned his company around. He returned to Kinsley for a guaranteed recital (at Trail's End) and another performance at the opera house—this time Shakespeare's *The Taming of the Shrew*. Charlie outlined his reasoning in a November 1909 column: "Realizing that if we would have the best dramatic attractions in Kinsley we as citizens must give them support." The plan worked. Gilmor continued to return twice in 1910 alone to Kinsley; the first time was for a social call and the second to perform his rendition of *Romeo and Juliet*. Gilmor again returned in 1911 when he performed at the glamorous and locally legendary wedding of Charlie's sister, Marion Edwards, and Jouett Shouse, an upstart businessman and aspiring politician from Kentucky. Up until this moment, the Edwards-Shouse wedding was the largest and most significant social and cultural event to occur in town. But the following year, based on a shared love of Shakespeare and a touring professional actor, that all changed.

Chapter 6

"Drama Capital of the West"

Charlie Edwards and Homegrown Talent

As time progressed into the second decade of the twentieth century, Charlie Edwards transposed Kinsley's love for the arts and performance from indoor venues into natural settings. With this idea, he formed the first permanent outdoor theater space in Kansas, the Meadowbrook Theatre. The productions featured massive casts of performers, at their peak reaching three hundred people on stage. Through these impressive and historically consequential gatherings, performers, storytellers and audiences defined a golden age of dramatic performance in small-town America.

Arkansas Valley Dramatic Festival Begins, 1912

In the spring of 1912, touring Shakespearean actor Gilmor Brown attempted to reorganize his approach to the theatrical business. Traveling companies like his, which journeyed from small town to small town, were struggling to make ends meet. The slowly increasing popularity of moving image shows, the "movies," started changing the entertainment landscape. With this in mind, Gilmor needed to find a sector of the theatrical industry where he could still make money, and he identified that with a rising national interest in community-based theater and pageantry. All Gilmor needed was the ideal community for such an endeavor. After nearly ten years roaming the United States and Canada, Gilmor picked up his pen and paper and addressed a letter to his friend in Kinsley, Kansas—a locale with decades of community performances behind it, not to mention a strong affinity for Shakespeare.

When Charlie Edwards received the letter from Gilmor Brown, he did not have to consider the proposition for long. This inquiry asked if he was interested in organizing a large-scale Shakespeare production, specifically the famous story of fairies and sprites *A Midsummer Night's Dream*, to be composed of local community members. It would utilize the latest cutting-edge theatrical theories. Charlie later recalled the moment as he considered mounting this undertaking: "As I looked out over a meadow on the banks of the Arkansas River, I seemed to suddenly see fairies skipping across the grass. That's how the thing was born." Charlie Edwards was not just an "organizer" of the event. He became its producer, coordinator and champion.

Before Gilmor arrived in Kinsley, Charlie hit the ground running. First, he organized a mission statement and vision for the enterprise and then formulated the event's name, the Arkansas Valley Dramatic Festival. Next, Charlie organized multiple layers of committees. He also recruited his brother-in-law, Jouett Shouse, as the festival's business manager. Due to Jouett's longtime connections with U.S. Speaker of the House Champ Clark, he had already risen to chairman of the Democratic caucus in his new home district. Jouett's financial and political resourcefulness and Charlie's connection with local clubs created a strong team, not to mention the financial backing of the wealthiest man in Edwards County, his father, Eugene Edwards. When Gilmor Brown arrived, the team was complete, and the festival was destined for success.

The press release sent out to newspapers across the state showcased the unbridled enthusiasm and ambitions of the Arkansas Valley Dramatic Festival:

> *A dream has been dreamed for western Kansas. Certain enthusiasts at Kinsley have long thought that our shortgrass country with its border memories, its sturdy present, and splendid possibilities is just the romantic locality which should foster the drama. This spring the dream crystalized into action. These persons have banded themselves together, have raised an ample financial support, and as a result of their faith in Kansans' love for the best in art and music, they are about to launch a new institution that is destined to significance in the art history of our state.*

The press release continued, exploring its novel setting and the sheer size of the cast, especially considering Kinsley's population (which had doubled in the last decade from approximately 700 to more than 1,500 people): "It will be presented, al fresco, on a sylvan stage of huge proportions, with a natural stream, immense old trees and a moonlight sky for scenery, by a company of one hundred persons."

Performing a play of this size outdoors was a first for Western Kansas. Nevertheless, the event was not promoted just for the nearby audiences, but rather for people around the state and region:

> *Kinsley's situation at the junction of the main line of the Santa Fe and the Hutchinson branch makes its train service excellent, and two fine new hotels, and numerous cafes, will furnish ample accommodations for visitors who desire to remain over night. The automobile roads leading to Kinsley are unsurpassed.*

On the day of the first performance, energy was in the air around Tenth Street and Briggs Avenue (which the rerouting of Coon Creek eventually reshaped in the 1930s). The audience reached this performance site, traveling in the latest automobiles, with horses and buggies, on the train and even on foot. Almost everyone involved in Kinsley's cultural and civic life was there: Eugene and Lizzie Edwards, Ed Noble and Jim Lewis; the poets were there too, with Cora Lewis, Ida Bostwick, Alice Erwin and Nell Woods. This group and five hundred other attendees brimmed with enthusiasm despite the unseasonably cold June weather. As the outdoor theater space filled with an anxious buzz, colorfully costumed townspeople waited in the wings between twinkling trees.

Music from a small orchestra reached the audience across a small brook that separated the onlookers from the action. In the meantime, a fairy legion, amassed behind the audience, began flitting down the center aisle to charm the gathering. This magical band congregated as the music played on; they filed onto a 150-foot stage lined with electric footlights shrouded in artificial shrubbery.

The music suddenly stopped as a flame-colored will-o'-the-wisp shot like an ember across a specially designed "fairy bridge," grasping the crowd's attention. This mythical sprite, played by local dancer Persis Colie dressed in oranges and reds, cackled in "elfin glee" while commanding the stage. Then, a trumpet sounded as the Athenian Duke Theseus entered with his betrothed, Hippolyta, and their many attendants. The two pairs of lovers entered the forest. Later, Charlie emerged into the sylvan surroundings, dressed in an extravagant tunic as Oberon, King

Above: The leads of Shakespeare's *A Midsummer Night's Dream* from the Arkansas Valley Dramatic Festival, June 1912. *Kinsley Public Library*.

Opposite, top: The program of Shakespeare's *A Midsummer Night's Dream* from the Arkansas Valley Dramatic Festival, June 1912. *Kinsley Public Library*.

Opposite, bottom: *The Ballad Monger* at Flohr's Opera House, one of the last productions staged there, November 1912; Charlie Edwards is at center. *Edwards County Historical Society*.

of the Fairies, quarreling with the Fairy Queen, played by Lucile DeTar; the named fairies followed them, and after them, eighty other individuals rounding out the massive pageant.

Kinsley's decades-long interest in Shakespeare had finally bloomed into one of the first Shakespeare festivals of its kind in the United States. On Sunday, June 9, one day after *A Midsummer Night's Dream* was slated to close, an extensive article celebrating Charlie and Gilmor's production appeared in the *Kansas City Star*. The paper produced nearly half a page, covered seven columns and contained four images—quite a spread for a small town three hundred miles from the metro paper. The reporter sent all those miles by train to investigate a potentially amateur-quality amateur Shakespeare production was smitten. The writer beamed with praise, describing the group they encountered on their trip in the best of terms:

> *Very often amateur performances are of interest only to the fathers and mothers of the performers, and from a dramatic standpoint they are likely to be very, very tragic. But it wasn't that way with Kinsley's outdoor play. There was a dash and a spirit about the performance that would have put many a professional effort to the blush.*

EDWARDS, NOBLE & CO.

Kinsley, :-: Kansas.

The Oldest, Largest and most Progressive Store in Edwards County.

"ONE PRICE TO ALL"

WILSON & ELY

Real Estate and Farm Loans

SHAFFER & SON

Implements and Hardware

J. O. HARNEY'S

Ice Cream Parlor—A Cool, Comfortable Place on a "MIDSUMMER NIGHT."

Purchasers of Ice Cream by the pint or quart go to HARNEY'S.

KINSLEY

Cleaning and Hat Works.

Cleaning, Pressing and Repairing. Ladies Work a Specialty.

All Work Guaranteed.

One Door West of Saddlerock Cafe

The Hard Handed Men of Athens.

Quince, A carpenter .... Mr. Kelton Lewis
Starveling, A tailor .... Mr. Edward H. Sellers
Snug, A joiner .... Mr. Wilbur Baxter
Flute, A bellows mender ...... Mr. Chester Baxter
Snout, A tinker .... Mr. Robert Von Zoll
Bottom, A weaver .... Mr. Gilmor Brown

FAIRIES

Oberon, King of the Fairies. Mr. Chas. R. Edwards
Titania, Queen of the Fairies . . Miss Lucile DeTar
Puck, Or Robin Goodfellow .... Miss Persis Colie

Peasblossom	ELVES	Master Fred Wilson
Cobweb		Master Gerome Wilson
Moth		Master William Beezley
Mustard Seed		Master Charles Beal

A Fairy .... Miss Dorothy Merryman

Fairies, elves, courtiers, guards, Amazons, priests, priestesses, vocal chorus and attendants to the NUMBER OF EIGHTY PERSONS.

The scene is a Fairy Wood near Athens.

NOTE:—There will be several short intermissions during which the orchestra will play the Mendelssohn "Midsummer Night's Dream" Music.

MRS. S. B. BELLOWS, MILLINERY.

Col. F. D. West

Veterinary Surgeon

Ex-President International Auctioneers' Association.

The Great Western Magnetic Auctioneer.

Kinsley, Kansas.

Fravel & Lewis

Feed and Produce

C. B. D. Colver

Real Estate and Insurance.

H. J. Wilson

Bonded Abstractor

Gilmor Brown's experience working with the renowned outdoor Shakespeare director Ben Greet certainly affected the final product, which the article's author pointed out. The reporter also covered details of the play's actions thoroughly but, most importantly, included the details of the community's reactions. It was not just for people "in town," but for the whole community. Farmers came in from the countryside with their animal teams and machinery, and guests came from hundreds of miles away. The *Kansas City Star* remarked:

> *Everybody believed in the play and wanted to see it succeed, and their wishes in that regard were amply gratified. The big outdoor theater was crowded every night. People went away and came again.... The whole community seemed to feel that it was not just "a play," but their play.*

The play had done what it was designed to do: create community pride, raise money for a local cause and bring people closer together. After completing what felt like a historic moment for Western Kansas, Charlie and Gilmor planned for "an institution" where they would give a festival-like Shakespeare play every summer. The *Star*'s piece closed with, "There seems to be no reason why that dream should not come true." Nearly two thousand people attended the three performances, five hundred more people than resided in town.

Gilmor left town to try his luck elsewhere after testing out his community Shakespeare festival idea. Meanwhile, Charlie and his team of theater-makers busily planned their next production with the communal energy working to their advantage. Kinsley school superintendent Daniel Baugher and Charlie began organizing a community production hosted by the local schools at Flohr's Opera House, titled *The Ballad Monger*. Charlie played the lead role as theatrical momentum continued.

JUSTIFYING THE DRAMATIC CENTER, 1913–1914

As the calendar changed to 1913, Kinsley's vibrant theatrical world was about to come to a screeching halt. The upcoming production of *Madame Butterfly* (that Charlie was organizing) had to be canceled. The current owner of Flohr's Opera House had to announce that he was shuttering the building due to structural safety concerns. After twenty-eight years and countless performances, the structure where Charlie stood throughout the two decades in recital after recital, and play after play, where he had seen his whole family perform in *Deestrick Skule*, had closed its doors.

Now, the only place to perform in Kinsley, at least with appropriate scenic considerations, was outdoors. One year after the trailblazing production, there was no promised second annual festival. However, this let-down was not on the minds of the people of Edwards County in the summer of 1913; a more pressing economic concern dominated the headlines as a wave of grasshoppers moved in to destroy crops. Still, the local press did not forget the dramatic glories of 1912, and a December 1913 *Hutchinson Gazette* article reported on Charlie's continuing plans: "It is the dream of his life to make the Arkansas Valley Dramatic Festival the big thing it seems likely to become."

With the closure of the opera house, the Kinsley Players needed a temporary space for indoor performance, so Charlie began work on a specially designed stage scaffolding inside the Congregational Church. Under Charlie's direction, the group mounted *Caprice*. Then, for the first time, they went on the road and toured the production around the immediate region to Spearville, Larned and St. John during February, March and April. After the exhibition, which received widely positive critical praise in all four towns, Charlie and his actors returned to Kinsley and performed with the high school to construct yet another play, *Mose*, in late April.

This exciting activity happened just months after Kinsley's thriving professional actor, the young and dauntless Lorin Raker, returned home to tell friends that he was off to Japan. The Universal Moving Picture Company now employed Lorin, and his hometown could not have been prouder. Charlie had succeeded in making Kinsley the "dramatic capital" of the West, and Lorin's career within the first generation of film actors was but one example.

Further confirmation of Kinsley's growing status appeared when Gilmor's letter arrived in late May, informing everyone of another event. This time, other cities wanted to be just like Kinsley: Hutchinson wanted its own festival. Gilmor Brown arrived and organized it, and Charlie and Lucile DeTar agreed to join and bolster the star power.

As the end of the Hutchinson *Twelfth Night* approached, the two festival producers channeled the energy from that accomplishment into providing a proper continuation of the Arkansas Valley Dramatic Festival. Charlie and Gilmor announced their community plans in the Edwards County papers. Through their considerable "hobnobbing" with each other, as the *Mercury* described it, the producing duo was ready to assemble their charitable

Charlie Edwards and his cast of *Caprice* in a publicity photo taken at his home, Trail's End, February 1914. *Edwards County Historical Society.*

cause (the Library Association), volunteer committees, community sponsors and creative teams. Charlie effectively served as producer, with Gilmor as director. They reasoned that the only way to move forward was to make it bigger and better than before, so the plans were initiated to double the number of actors to two hundred participants.

While this play did not call for the renowned fairies of its predecessor, there was a novel component nonetheless. Desiring a high degree of authenticity, Charlie requested goats and sheep to appear in the pastoral scenes. Meanwhile, the costuming committee searched for appropriate animal skins used for the country characters, like the shepherd Silvius, who was being played by Charlie's new right-hand man, Tom Mairs. The recent high school graduate had taken a lead role in the high school's adaptation of *The Merchant of Venice* and played in the acclaimed *Caprice* production months earlier. The Mairs family had been a fixture in Kinsley for almost a decade, and Tom, like his older brother Chester, was becoming increasingly active in the local arts scene. In addition to playing Silvius, he collaborated with Charlie on the advertising committee and with Gilmor on scenic design, as he had done with *Midsummer*.

The stage where Tom assembled the set differed from the festival's original incarnation. At last, after decades of consistent theatrical activity, this year, the production inaugurated a new outdoor playhouse, a first for the state of Kansas. Charlie worked with local contractor Roy Hatfield to construct a stage and grandstands that held seven hundred people on the outskirts of town along the creek, on land owned by his father, Eugene Edwards. Every location on the grandstand was to "command a perfect view," as the *Graphic* noted on August 13, 1914. The platform-style stage itself was one hundred feet wide but only a few inches off the ground and surrounded by trees on three sides. Charlie also envisioned that this outdoor space would be an ideal location for community meetings and gatherings of all purposes and ensured that it was "substantial" enough to remain part of his permanent institution. After all, as described in the papers, it was the "second annual" festival. It seems the desire for permanency in the institution overshadowed the inconvenient truth that it was not annual, having missed 1913. Nevertheless, with an outdoor theater now part of the town's infrastructure, surely the festival was to continue.

Soon enough, after long days of rehearsal, logistics and promotions, the opening day of the four-day festival arrived. The town bustled with activity as people disembarked the trains, parked their automobiles and filled hotels and local eateries, and merchants decorated their storefronts to attract customers. Beck's Boy Band played in the streets and also at the production's opening. While the grandstands were "comfortably full," fortunately for the quickly assembled structure, its maximum of seven hundred people never gathered on a single night.

While Charlie and Gilmor tried to reach 200 participants (not counting sheep and goats), it's unclear if they did, as one report only lists 150. Other sources insist it was 200. Regardless of the number of participants, with the inauguration of the new theater and well over 100 costumed actors, Charlie claimed in the papers that it was the "largest and most elaborate production ever made in the state." The *Hutchinson News* agreed, noting on August 14 that Kinsley's festival had "become a widely known institution in the Short Grass country."

All of the activity predictably aroused even more press. On August 20, the hometown team at the *Graphic* proclaimed the festival "as epoch-making" as 1912's *Midsummer*, while the *Great Bend Tribune* predicted coming national fame. Likewise, the *Larned Chronoscope* noted how ambitious the project was even for a town "many times as large" as Kinsley and could not believe that the "financial returns approach the actual expense involved." Fortunately for all involved, unlike many other theatrical endeavors, there was no necessity to break even. The project celebrated Kinsley and its dedication to arts and culture, an aspect that even the most fastidious businessmen embraced. It was now quite clear that theater could bring economic activity to the town. Kinsley now had the structures in place; all it needed was the continual support to make the festival a lasting institution, or as the *Mercury* described on August 27, a "permanent fixture."

THE PROFESSIONAL TOUR, 1915

Change in the Edwards family dynamics affected Kinsley's theatrical offerings in 1915. Lizzie Edwards was beginning to drift more often and farther away from her husband, Eugene. This also worked well for Charlie, who, despite his great love for Kinsley and all accomplished in town, was being seduced by the allure of the professional stage in Kansas City. He secured professional acting opportunities in the city and interacted with other up-and-coming actors.

When he returned to Kinsley in June 1915, Charlie had caught the professional fever and wanted to exhibit this newfound energy to Western Kansas. Charlie and his mixed company of professionals from Kansas City and amateurs from Kinsley played locally with Oscar Wilde's *The Importance of Being Ernest*. Then this group toured four other local towns, even scheduling a performance close to Hutchinson in Lyons, which was later canceled. Charlie did not take his company into Hutchinson, where Gilmor busily prepared his amateur cast for yet another *Midsummer Summer Night's Dream* (the 1912 production in Kinsley began a trend that continued to pop up around Western Kansas).

When Charlie's great professional tour of Western Kansas was completed, the only organizing energy left was enough to picnic with a 50 percent nonlocal cast at his Meadowbrook Theatre. So, again, there was no Shakespeare festival, even after the continued and sustained marketing about its glories and institutional status. The director's zeal for professionalism seemed to have gotten the best of him. Dignified local ideals were placed aside for a moment of sophisticated indulgence—a touring semiprofessional was a greater accomplishment than a home-talent festival, or at least that was the conventional wisdom. However, it was not true. The metro and local papers were far more interested in Kinsley's productions.

More of these "highbrow" theatricals were to come for Charlie; news of a new cutting-edge semiprofessional group in New York City, the Washington Square Players, had made its way through the national press in publications like *Vanity Fair*. Charlie must have seen their exhilaratingly innovative work covered in abundant detail. He wanted to be a part of it. So, he packed his bags and caught a train for New York. There, throughout 1916's first half, Charlie performed in this renowned theater company, taking a leading role in its world premiere of *The Red Cloak*. Then he performed again in one of New York City's largest-ever productions, the Shakespeare-inspired *Caliban and the Yellow Sands*, written by theatrical theoretician Percy MacKaye, which featured thousands of amateur actors led by a star-studded professional cast. This massive show was the culmination of the "Shakespeare Tercentenary" and celebration of the 300th anniversary of the playwright's death. For several scenes, with an audience of more than ten thousand, Kinsley's own Charlie Edwards took center stage.

SHAKESPEARE IN THE SHORT GRASS, 1916

While Charlie initially tinkered with the idea of resting during his summer trip at home in Kinsley, friends lobbied for a return of the Arkansas Valley Dramatic Festival. Especially after hearing of the many events happening throughout the country in Shakespeare's honor, Kinsley's dramatic enthusiasts were salivating at the opportunity to return to the Meadowbrook Theatre.

Local theatrical interest was as high as ever, even in Charlie's absence. As he basked in the theatrical incubator of communal theater–crazed New York City, his colleagues, students and fans in Kansas continued. Their previous work together had inspired them to never stop. Lucile DeTar,

Persis Colie and several other Edwards protégés spent the early part of the year performing professionally with the Santa Fe Railroad. Colie also enjoyed the previous fall season with Gilmor Brown, impressing him with her abilities and resolve. Gilmor had remained in Hutchinson in his most recent attempt to find a place to settle, producing several plays and opening a School of Expression. Charlie was proud that Persis Colie had worked with Gilmor's company. It must have seemed like another feather in his cap. So now, the time seemed right to convince Charlie Edwards to revive Kinsley's theatrical "institution."

Charlie's friends did not have to overexert their persuasive abilities. Within a few days, Charlie announced that he planned to stage another Shakespeare play at Kinsley's Meadowbrook Theatre. Lucile DeTar signed on as his assistant director, and together they assembled what they claimed to be the largest (by size of the cast) production of *Twelfth Night* in "theatrical history," a distinction difficult to disprove. The duo selected three hundred people this time, representing around one-fifth of the town's population. Kinsley was transformed into a city-wide theatrical workshop for the third time in five years. Rehearsals were held on the lawn at Trail's End. Notices

An advertisement for Kinsley's production of Shakespeare's *Twelfth Night*, August 1916. *From the* Kinsley Mercury, *Edwards County Historical Society*.

were issued for people to lend their animals to the production, featuring a medieval hunting pageant. Kinsley's largest-ever spectacle was supercharged by Charlie's recent experience in New York, which mobilized droves of people. Lucile DeTar took the lead role of Viola while assistant directing.

Having played Orsino in Hutchinson and Valentine in New York City, this time Charlie took the role of Malvolio and prepared to don yellow cross-gartered stockings. The visuals were assembled by longtime Kinsley set designer Gus Hann, who found a few minutes to leave his critical role as postmaster to help create the necessary pieces for the scenic layout at the Meadowbrook. For the music, Charlie contracted a Hutchinson orchestra. Unchecked inspiration abounded. If Kinsley's festival had an equal in size, scope and vision somewhere in the United States, no one had heard of it.

The press realized the organization's value to the state and the region. Hannah Mitchell, a popular *Kansas City Star* columnist, appeared in Kinsley for the opening of the four-day festival. As the production closed, the *Star* released an exclusive, "Shakespeare in the Short Grass Country," reminding Kansas Citians that this remote, little-known town had a cultural treasure they did not. Charlie mentioned Gilmor in the interview, and his name appeared with the first festival. However, most crucially, the latest iteration of the Arkansas Valley Dramatic Festival was being recognized as an institution by the state. Kansas's lieutenant governor, William Yoast Morgan, released a statement praising Charlie and Kinsley in a *Hutchinson News* article titled "Our Kansas Festival" on August 1, 1916. He wrote in part:

> *Mr. Edwards has had great success in New York City as an actor, and his talents have been applauded in many other cities, but to our mind his most wonderful achievement is the inspiration he has given at Kinsley.... Associated with him are others who have caught the spirit from their leader and as a result Kinsley is known far and wide for dramatic festivals.*

Charlie's vision succeeded in reimagining American theater in Kansas. Year after year, community members and local organizational structures supported his ventures. Furthermore, he facilitated professionally trained leadership that developed the talent of fully amateur casts with a spirit of collective responsibility. Lastly, the festival developed a new form of regional theater that MacKaye had envisioned in his ambitions for pageantry. Now, statewide officials joined the civic pride, marketing the productions to the region as a whole. The work was unprecedented for the community arts organizations and pointed toward a future of nonprofit institutions.

Some of the "fairies" from Kinsley's 1912 production of Shakespeare's *A Midsummer Night's Dream* pose for a photo. *Kinsley Public Library*.

Still, it meant much more than these distant theories or constructs to the people of Kinsley. It was *their* festival. Ten days after *Hutchinson News* printed the lieutenant governor's endorsement of Kansas's festival, the paper returned to praise Kinsley for this impressive undertaking:

> *A town which gives so notable and so cultural an offering to the state each year is bound to rank high among our cities. Parents with children to educate will be eager to settle in a community known far and wide for its ability to educate and inspire the minds and souls of youth. Meanwhile, do not delay. Load up your car and run over to Kinsley before* [Shakespeare's] Twelfth Night *ceases to be a reality and becomes merely a lovely, haunting memory in the annals of our state.*

Charlie Edwards found himself engaged to direct more Shakespeare in Kinsley before he could return to New York City to perform during the winter season. The momentum in Kinsley could not be stopped. The high school asked him to present on Shakespeare's *Macbeth*, and he obliged. Seventeen years earlier, fresh out of oratory school in Kansas City, he had performed this same play, solo, in town, and he always relished a revival. Since the occasion had arisen and Charlie was still home, the school board wanted to benefit from his expertise and celebrity. The board asked him to do the annual play for the high school.

As Charlie prepared for his next play, Shakespeare's *The Comedy of Errors*, to honor his fellow educators, he threw an extravagant musical party at Trail's End and sent out more than one hundred invitations. All of Kinsley's arts areas collided at one event. Poetry readings and music by Persis Colie, Josephine Hills and Ida Bostwick delighted the crowds, and Lucile DeTar appeared in her costume from the summer's *Twelfth Night*. Edwards County could not get enough Shakespeare, theater, poetry, music and community. In the coming days, *The Comedy of Errors* charmed and entertained the audiences in Kinsley and neighboring Ford County, specifically in Spearville, for its new school building's inaugural performance.

The performers could not have known that the *Comedy of Errors* production was the final live Shakespeare performance of the 1910s and the end of an era. From 1906 to 1916, residents in Kinsley saw eleven full-length Shakespeare plays, a cultural offering that only a metropolitan city could rival: two professional productions of *Romeo and Juliet*, along with professional productions of *The Merchant of Venice*, *The Taming of Shrew*, *As You Like It* and *Julius Caesar*. Kinsley High School produced two, *The Merchant of Venice* and *The Comedy of Errors*, while *A Midsummer Night's Dream*, *As You Like It* and *Twelfth Night* were presented as three large-scale productions during the Arkansas Valley Dramatic Festival. Despite this seemingly unstoppable trend, the world was about to change, and so would Kinsley's entertainment tastes.

THEATER DURING WAR AND PANDEMIC YEARS, 1917–1920

On April 2, 1917, Marion Edwards Shouse ascended the staircase in the bustling U.S. Capitol Building in Washington, D.C. Her husband, Congressman Jouett Shouse of Kinsley, took his seat on the floor of the House. They looked on as President Wilson, recently reelected on an anti-war platform, arrived in the chamber to ask Congress for a declaration of war. Marion watched from the House chamber's balcony and leaned over

Charlie Edwards's publicity portrait for the Harlequin Players by Kansas City photographers Orville Hixon and James Hargis Connelly, 1917. *Edwards County Historical Society.*

the railing as the president spoke. The speech was influential; four days later, the United States declared war on the German empire.

It was not long before Charlie heard his sister's firsthand account of the war declaration. Along with this news came a steady stream of wartime restrictions and adaptations. So, Charlie concocted an idea for what entertainment could look like during a time of adversity. The performing arts had always been such an integral part of Kinsley's cultural life; they could not stop, even for war. After returning from founding a "Little Theatre" in Kansas City alongside Tom Mairs, Charlie assembled a company of Kinsley actors and called them the Community Players, likely because they performed in a small movie theater called the "Community Theatre." Next, he established his cause as a Red Cross benefit and donated 25 percent of his earnings to its efforts. The rest of the money was used to fund the production itself. He merged his theatrical offerings with films at the town's moviehouse. Charlie reasoned that if he joined these two types of entertainment, he might have to spend less time assembling the work. His cast performed a one-act play and then played a short moving picture.

With Tom Mairs's continued assistance, in 1917, Charlie rounded up local actors still in town as he awaited the thrilling opening of Kinsley's cutting-edge entertainment center, the Palace Theatre. Persis Colie joined the company along with Ruby Raker, Lorin's sister (Lorin was busily working on his largest film yet on sets in far-flung locales). First, the group presented *The Price of Orchids*, which had to be relabeled as "not a benefit" because regulations dictated that 100 percent of the funds needed to go to the Red Cross. Still, in Charlie's mind, it was no matter that the show itself failed to meet the standards for the benefit. After all, Kinsley in total, raised $5,100, a significant amount at the time.

Still, there was more work to be done. Immediately after the Red Cross work, influential school board members, including Superintendent

Daniel Baugher, again approached Charlie and inquired if he wanted to direct another production. It was the first time he could produce a play in Kinsley's newest theatrical facility, the Palace Theatre. Charlie determined that for such an occasion, his hometown's first "modern staging," he would reach into the past and retrieve an eighteenth-century British play, *The Good-Natur'd Man*.

This play satisfied one primary purpose. Charlie used his collection of costumes he had acquired for his 1914 production of *Caprice*. This strategy was necessary to win over his audience and shield him from criticism. Since the costumes were already purchased for the earlier production, they were palatable to the thrifty social trends sweeping the nation. Right away, Charlie made it clear in his statement to the *Graphic* that he was not "infringing upon the war-time economy" with the production on November 22, 1917. Likewise, his congressman brother-in-law had recently, along with Marion, held a "war-time dinner" at Trail's End meant to set an excellent example of food conservation. If the wealthiest and most influential family in town were rationing, everyone else must also. Another generation of Kinsley actors emerged with this play: Sue Bidwell took the leading role, and Gracia Beeler provided the musical accompaniment. There seemed to be no slowing of the near half-century theater tradition in the small town. Inspiration still hung in the air, and it seemed that not even war could stop the momentum.

As the draftees and volunteers amassed at Camp Funston, a consequential moment in world history also altered Kinsley's trajectory. A flu epidemic traced back to Western Kansas tore through military bases and, consequently, was exported throughout the world as the soldiers were deployed. Charlie and his team of performers from Edwards County did not end up at the base to entertain the troops—not because of the spread of the virus, but rather because he came down with appendicitis and was taken in for an emergency operation in Kansas City. Meanwhile, back home in Kinsley, Mayor Ben Ely Sr. announced the closure of schools to stop the spread of the disease. He also issued a memo enforcing strict quarantine procedures. Churches were closed and public meetings were banned, including at the newly opened Palace Theatre, which remained shuttered for months.

As Kinsley and the rest of the country recovered from this devastating influenza pandemic and the Great War ended, Charlie Edwards relocated again to New York City, where he took up residence at the Algonquin Hotel. There he fraternized with the most well-known columnists, playwrights, critics and artists of the emerging Jazz age. In between flu outbreaks, Charlie also had the opportunity to see the world's best theater and the chance to see his onetime protégé and Kinsley High School graduate, Lorin Raker, in his first starring role in a major film, Émile Chautard's 1919 *The Mystery of the Yellow Room*.

By the next year, the pandemic was in the past, and a former Kinsley resident summoned Charlie to Okmulgee, Oklahoma, to lead yet another revival of the renowned 1912 *A Midsummer Night's Dream*. The magic of that production nearly a decade earlier still loomed in the minds of many, even though theatrical tastes were changing; the coming advent of the "talkies" only reinforced this change. Nevertheless, women's clubs, theater organizations and literary groups in the region still wanted to re-create Kinsley's famed performance.

As Charlie Edwards and Lorin Raker worked in the theater industry in New York City and Hollywood, back in Kinsley, Tom Mairs picked up the mantle and continued the high-quality theater. Tom worked diligently on his second play for the high school; he was proud of what he had accomplished. The rookie director wanted his mentor to see it and encouraged Charlie to visit. The *Graphic* trumpeted "the producer and actor who put Kinsley on the theatrical map in years gone by" to indicate the now-famous director's return to Kinsley in 1920.

The article described how the twenty-five-year-old Tom Mairs had received all his theatrical training under Charlie. Together, the pair assembled a light comedy, *Green Stockings*, to be performed at the Palace Theatre. The *Lewis Press* showered Charlie in praise, calling him "the greatest director that Kansas has ever known, in fact one of the best known directors of amateur plays in America." Charlie reciprocated the praise, informing the public that "[i]t is more fun to do a play here [in Kinsley] than anywhere else." While Shakespeare had vanished, high-quality artistic plays had made it through a world war and a pandemic; this type of entertainment seemed here to stay.

END OF THE EDWARDS ERA, 1920–1926

During the early 1920s, Tom Mairs led most locally assembled dramatic activities in Kinsley, but when Charlie Edwards returned to collaborate with his former acolyte, he also announced a unique and novel program, the Charles Edwards Junior Players. This program was meant to emulate similar activities he had observed in the cities as it had "become a prominent feature of educational activities." The directors cast seventeen children to play in the first production, *The Fairy Fantasy*. Notably, the children who participated in Charlie's next pixie production were not even born when Kinsley transformed into Fairyland in 1912. The world had changed thoroughly in a dozen years, but Charlie's desire to bring that same theatrical magic to Kinsley had not. Yet another generation could benefit from these communal passions.

Along with his peers, twelve years earlier, Jerome "Jerry" Wilson had donned what looked like hooded onesie pajamas and took the stage with the dueling King and Queen of the Fairies. Now approaching his twenty-third birthday, Jerry still participated in the productions. He had gone from background fairy in *Midsummer* to leading man in the previous fall's *Billeted.* Now he joined the long-running club and welcomed familiar faces back to town for visits like Lucile DeTar and Persis Colie. The productions were more than just entertainment or diversions from daily life—they were a shared connection to an earlier time. These performances evoked cherished memories, which is why Charlie fancied returning the fairies from the fabled 1912 production to the stage in his educational presentation of *The Fairy Fantasy*.

The productions also looked to the future. Charlie and his new assistant director, Sue Bidwell, programmed Susan Glaspell's *Suppressed Desires* (the directing duo also included another light comedy, *Bank Holiday*, in which assistant director Sue starred). Only ten years earlier, this play was "too special" for the Washington Square Players in New York's most progressive neighborhood. Now, this playlet appeared at the Palace Theatre in Kinsley; amateur theater makers had changed the way America thought of theater. While performing *Suppressed Desires* demonstrated progress, *The Fairy Fantasy* was not like the glorious reminiscence of 1912 *Midsummer* that inspired it. Perhaps some memories could never be relived. Still, the future of theatrical excellence in Kinsley had not been abandoned. In August 1924, Charlie shared another even more ambitious dream in the *Mercury*, the same paper he had once owned and edited more than a decade and a half earlier:

> *There has long been strong within me a hope that someday I might give Kinsley a resident stock company, composed of amateurs, highly trained as actors, who for love of the work, of the nurture of their own talents, and of the pleasure they can give their friends and fellow citizens, might from time to time, act honestly written dramas of various kinds.... Audiences which crowd houses as ours have been crowded to see plays of this sort, are an unending encouragement to director and actors. To fail them would be unpardonable.*

With his latest mission in print, the now forty-three-year-old director pressed on.

A publicity photo of Don Cook by renowned entertainment photographer James Hargis Connelly, circa 1925. *Collection of William Floyd Wolfgang.*

Through his recent engagements that culminated at the Kansas City Theater's season-end banquet, Charlie met rising amateur Don Cook. He offered the up-and-coming local Kansas City actor sufficiently enticing financial incentives to make the trip out to Kinsley and perform in his production of *Clarence* at the Palace Theatre. Cook embraced the opportunity to learn from the veteran producer and to call himself a semiprofessional actor. After all, *Clarence* was only the fourth play he had ever performed. He was still a very green amateur, but Charlie's publicity treatment transformed him into a star. The *Mercury* proclaimed that *Clarence* was the best play in Kinsley in a decade.

High on the triumphant reviews, Charlie secured Cook's participation in the next production just weeks after *Clarence*. He had produced more plays since July than he ever had in Kinsley within one year. The final selection was George Arliss's *The Molusc*. Now, Don Cook had played as many lead roles in Kinsley as he had in Kansas City. Charlie had given his career the educational boost that he could acquire in few other places.

By the mid-1920s, Kinsley, by this time a small city of about two thousand people, had launched the careers of two Hollywood actors, two consequential theater producers and many other regional theater stars. In 1925, Charlie Edwards received an offer from the Tulsa Little Theatre to be the first full-time (professional) director of its amateur productions. He was an instant local celebrity within the theater circles. Some found him to be as "smooth as glass" and "sensitive," while others took "eccentric" one step further, labeling him "exotic." With all his idiosyncrasies and years of experience, he successfully led the Tulsa Little Theatre through a crucial, formative year of its development.

However, Charlie Edwards's lifelong battle with severe depression caught up to him. On June 1, 1926, a growing despondency intersected with a long-running feud with his father, Eugene, and Charlie took his own life, overdosing on a prescription sedative in Tulsa. Newspapers across the country from

New York to Texas carried the story of his death under poignant headlines like "Artist's Yearning for Love Is Blamed in Death by Poison," but it was far too close to home for his friends in Kinsley. Despite his wishes to be buried in his hometown, Charlie Edwards was laid to rest at a Kansas City cemetery.

After Charlie's death, the theatrical environment in Kinsley began to shift from a consistent flow of performances to one more typical of a town its size. Moreover, the world was to change yet again. The Great Depression was only three years away, and the ravages of the Dust Bowl were yet to come. Still, Kinsley's golden age of performing arts left an impact far exceeding the Edwards County line.

Chapter 7

"Surpasses Descriptive Power"

Musical Performance

Like Kinsley's literary and dramatic landscape, its musical dimension surprised residents and visitors alike. From the magic of a mysterious vagabond violinist to the rich harmonies of the Women's Chorus, the critics and audiences often lacked the necessary vocabulary to describe the concerts they experienced. As with the other art forms, the music bound them together, not just with the harmonies but also with the feeling of community.

Locally based music organizations began as early as the 1870s and flourished into groups known throughout the state. While some musicians rehearsed together, others traveled to Europe by steamship to receive a world-class music education. Two composers emerged from Kinsley's small population and published sheet music for the rapidly evolving music industry. Amid this musical energy, Kinsley hosted opera festivals at its cherished opera house before time ushered in the Jazz Age.

Vagabond and Touring Musicians, 1878–1899

In the early years, one could never predict what traveling entertainer or charlatan might get off the train and try to make a dollar or two with a street routine. These performances were often lost to time because they were nothing beyond the everyday ephemera. However, now and then, fate traded a commonplace street musician for the drama of mystery and intrigue.

According to two Kinsley papers, on the morning of December 10, 1879, a "poorly but neatly clad" stranger walked into town and stood on Kinsley's frosty streets. With a rubber cloth violin case strapped to his back, this short man with "light hair mingled with gray" commenced preaching and lecturing from the streets. Considering the icy temperature, fluctuating radically throughout the week, the size of the crowd the stranger amassed was impressive. Word of the stranger's rhetoric, vocal delivery and simple presence quickly spread through Kinsley.

However, a local lawyer and his associates were not about to let the citizenry fall victim to a vagabond charlatan. Thinking that he may be a raving lunatic (who wanders into town from the vast empty prairie and tries his hand at street performing in the freezing grip of December), several in this group attempted to tease him with jeers and asides. The *Edwards County Leader* recorded that the stranger's replies were "ever ready" and that the "laugh was always at the expense of the would-be ridiculer." This man was not the average "wandering street speaker," one viewer recalled, as he also tackled most of the day's political issues and religious topics. With opportunities for traveling performances so scarce, local business leaders, likely including Ed Noble, paid for and organized an impromptu lecture at Calkins Hall. The stranger consented. Noble's amateur acting associate Andy Erwin was selected to introduce the man to the crowd.

The only problem that remained was how to bill the evening. The stranger had not revealed his name to anyone in the several hours he had been there, and one questioner did not have luck uncovering information. "Who are you?" they asked. The stranger stuck to his persona: "It matters not. I have a mission to fill; in doing so, I act in accordance with my best judgment the power and qualification God has given me."

Excitement and intrigue snowballed. The man was no longer the "the stranger" but had received another name, bestowed on him by his adoring fans: "the Unknown." Even with only hours' notice on a blustery cold night, nearly one hundred people filed into the hall and paid a fifteen-cent admission. There were no recorded complaints this night of seating or loud boys or itinerant drunks. That night, the Kinsley audience sat, craving more intrigue from the Unknown. Andy Erwin stepped forward and presented the nameless man who could not be introduced.

The Unknown began his "sermon," which was no longer about politics like earlier in the day but rather almost entirely on novel ideas within Christianity. The *Edwards County Leader* declared his message was "interesting," but that his street delivery was stronger. Meanwhile, the

Valley Republican disagreed and provided a nuanced review and account of the man's curious performance:

> *His delivery, when not playing the role of the awkward—by throwing his coat tails in front of his arms as he shoved his hands into his pockets, or rubbing his eyes, or holding his hands before his face—was good; breaking from these spells, he would ascend a flight of eloquence, displaying his wonderful power of elocution.*

After he concluded his impromptu speech, the Unknown gave a "truly grand" recitation of an unnamed Edgar Allan Poe poem, undoubtedly catching the attention of Kinsley's aspiring poets. Still, there was more to come; the orator had saved his strongest message for last. He took out his violin. At this moment, both critics' responses returned to unanimous and strong praise; the music presented to the audience "surpassed [their] descriptive power." Then, after his performance, he lightly received his audience before checking into the Kinsley Hotel with his freshly earned six dollars.

The next morning, Kinsley awoke still abuzz, fueled with ongoing intrigue over the Unknown. The idea of having him stay in town for another speech so they could learn more of him grew so great that he was enticed to remain at least one more day. A considerable sum of money was presented in advance to try to persuade him to remain for another performance at Calkins Hall. The Unknown's response was simple: "Satan, get thee behind me!"

The Unknown grabbed his violin and began walking away from town into the vast, freezing prairie. The temperature was four degrees Fahrenheit. Those seeking additional information on him went to the hotel to see if they might learn anything else about his one-night stay. The proprietor did have the first and only piece of information. The mysterious orator checked in under the name Lucius Alstone of San Francisco.

However, this information did not help solve the mystery at that time, and it remains so a century and a half later. This name or variations of it yield no results in today's newspaper and ancestry databases and other search tools. Furthermore, in the area surrounding Kinsley, there is no record of another wandering, violin-playing orator in the months before and after this incident. Lucius Alstone, or the name locals gave him, the Unknown, walked into Kinsley from nowhere and back into that void.

Reluctant to move on from a perfectly delicious mystery, the *Valley Republican* concluded its sizable coverage of the event with an appropriate amount of entertaining gravitas:

> *Who this man is, where he came from, and where he has gone, is a mystery that we may never solve; but that he is a man with a history, if known would be interesting; a man with powers of speech and ability that would, if in a proper channel, carry him to a degree of eminence, is certain.*

Lucius Alstone was but one name on a long list of performers who passed through Kinsley during these years. As Flohr's Opera House became the premier performance venue in town, finding quality performers became a perennial problem. Not every street urchin turned out to be a violin virtuoso. Sometimes the performances did not meet the high standards of the local clubs and societies. If there was a problem with a performer, locals took up the matter with the in-house manager. After a few complaints arose with this method, various clubs eventually developed committees to pass judgment on performers' suitability. Consequently, when wandering guitarist and "Edison's talking machine" owner Professor Frank Graves Robertson (1862–1944) reappeared in newspaper announcements, only intrigue arose. Professor Robertson had previously passed muster from the "merit committee" in March 1886 during his first visit to town, so his reemergence was met with nothing but welcome.

Professor Robertson became well liked in Kinsley, and his first visit, when he was twenty-four years old, was one of his earliest performances in Kansas. This 1886 show inaugurated a decade-long career touring across the Sunflower State and then returning to his native Missouri. Robertson possessed the abilities of a natural musical performer and, he might have argued, a savant. He perfected his one-man-band routine, which initially began with five instruments at once. But his penchant for performance did not end there. He also had a keen interest in emerging technologies, especially those developed by Thomas Edison, from lightbulbs to phonographs. Earlier in his youth, in the late 1870s, Robertson wrote to Edison directly and told him that he was experimenting with "ten cell batteries" and carbon sticks and "wanted to know if it would light his glove light." Ten days later, a "bulb the size of your thumb" arrived in the mail from Edison with no note or explanation (as Robertson later recalled in the February 14, 1929 edition of the *Springfield Leader*). The bulb worked. After that point, the one-man band added Edison's inventions to his acts.

When Professor Robertson returned to Flohr's Opera House in 1888, he had just wrapped a successful two-week-long residency in Wichita. With him, he brought seven instruments, two more than last time: guitar, mandolin, violoncello, tambourine, violin, harmonica and triangle. The accounts indicate that he somehow played them all at once and then exhibited the phonograph. Robertson made an explanation of the technology that was "so simple that all the children [were] able to understand it." With fifteen-cent adult tickets, the crowds poured into the opera house to catch the multitalented performer.

Kinsley again had the opportunity to have Frank Robertson back at the opera house for a third time in August 1891. The Ladies Society at the Congregational Church had heard that Robertson expanded his act, yet again, to include "genuine hypnotism" and legerdemain—with Spiritualist or "occult science" practices becoming more popular, this was an appealing act to the group's membership. He was now billed as a one-man-band mesmerist. Still, because Robertson was, in many ways, the exemplar from an era of performing fabulists, he determined that those two very different acts might not sufficiently fill a night's entertainment. With that in mind, he purchased automatons, humanoid figures that moved automatically by winding gears, and coupled them with his phonographs to construct what he billed as "multilingual automatons." One of them, possibly due to its elemental composition, he styled the "Iron Man."

Robertson's most memorable act, and final in Kinsley, was his hypnotism attempt on three local volunteers. The *Graphic* commendably chronicled the event:

> *Two of the three subjects selected were not susceptible to the professor's power, but the third apparently became completely under his control. At the command of the professor he struck a match and attempted to set fire to an imaginary hornet's nest. The frantic efforts made by the susceptible subject to fight off the hornets that, to his distorted imagination, were toying with his whiskers, were exceedingly amusing and elicited shouts of laughter.*

The "Professor" knew that audience participation reliably paid off, and this newspaper review only increased curiosity and entertainment value. The Professor was a musician, scientist and entertainer, all wrapped into one. Frank Robertson attuned his performances to what audiences wanted, and with his talent, he earned a living.

EARLY HOMEGROWN MUSIC ORGANIZATIONS, 1878–1899

While Lucius Alstone and Frank Robertson were among the most memorable characters to tour through Kinsley in the late nineteenth century, they were part of a group of professional musicians who blended musical performance with other forms of entertainment. A more common and widely embraced approach to musical performance placed local people on center stage. These groups had a solid foundation and had existed since Kinsley's earliest years. In the 1870s, the Kinsley String band performed for religious functions and public lectures. The Kinsley Brass Band, sometimes known as the Kinsley Cornet Band, also performed significant functions like the meeting of the Soldiers and Sailors Union at Gem Hall, as the *Edwards County Leader* chronicled on May 30, 1878. These groups combined forces with the Glee Club for Fourth of July celebrations in the 1870s.

These locally based music ensembles continued throughout the 1880s and 1890s. The groups not only assembled to play together, but they also collectively owned their own instruments and lent them out to the musicians. For example, in March 1884, the *Graphic* reported that the Kinsley String Band had purchased a new cello of "superior tone" for the ensemble. Like nonprofit organizations today, the Kinsley Cornet Band asked the citizens of Kinsley to support the endeavor with financial contributions. At the time of this request, printed in the *Mercury* on August 8, 1885, the band had a membership of twenty-two musicians and had secured the services of "one of the most competent instructors in the west." The band performed at community functions such as the Edwards County Fair as early as 1885.

The musical groups represented community progress and cooperation. As such, Kinsley's instrumental and vocal ensembles performed together, such as the oratorio *Queen Esther*, which took place at Flohr's Opera House on November 11 and 12, 1885. Moreover, the success of these musical groups was not isolated from the community's overall growth. In March 1887, the "boom year," the Kinsley Band announced that "the members practice regularly and propose to advance with the boom." However, the boom year did not pan out as some predicted, and as times turned difficult for many, the band scheduled fewer and fewer performances. By April 11, 1889, the *Mercury* had printed this message, "What has become of the Kinsley Cornet Band? We don't hear them 'toot' anymore," and publicly tried to reenergize their efforts. The band did return in various iterations during the 1890s.

Also during this time, a group of around twenty Kinsley women led by Cora Lewis assembled into a Ladies Chorus. These groups had become

The Kinsley Ladies Chorus' comic opera production of *The Dress Rehearsal*, featuring Cora Lewis in a lead role, February 1897. *Kinsley Public Library*.

popular around the state, and since Kinsley never wanted to lack any recent cultural and performance trends, an organization was assembled. The group's accompanist was eighteen-year-old Gertrude Pearson, daughter of one of Kinsley's physicians, Dr. Prince Albert Pearson. The group's most widely publicized event arrived in February 1897 with the performance of a comic opera titled *The Dress Rehearsal: A Musical Sketch* at Flohr's Opera House under the direction of Hutchinson music teacher Henry Rudesill (1873–1953).

The Dress Rehearsal comic opera sets up a play-within-a-play scenario by creating an imitation of *Cinderella*; it proved very popular with audiences, as described in the February 26, 1897 edition of the *Graphic*. While the production was considered "some miles below Shakespeare," it was wholly enjoyed by participants and the community alike. The excitement over the production was so significant that a photographer was summoned to the opera house to stage a rare cast photo. The Kinsley Ladies Chorus production of *The Dress Rehearsal* remains the earliest extant photo of a Kinsley performance of any kind and set the stage for future shows in the decades to come. This production also boosted the teaching career of the director, Henry Rudesill, who was preparing for his second summer teaching piano, organ and guitar in Kinsley. After the summer of 1897 teaching in town, Rudesill went on to the Oberlin Conservatory of Music and made his career teaching, performing and writing music in Hutchinson. He performed at the 1915 World's Fair in San Francisco on a new form of player piano and also published several pieces of music.

KINSLEY'S GOLDEN AGE OF PERFORMANCE, 1900–1925

For years, large-scale performances of Kinsley's amateur singers, musicians and actors remained a favorite musical form. By the turn of the century, special events also signaled a new era. On May 18, 1906, a regionally influential group of business leaders, members of the Kansas City Commercial Club, visited Kinsley. This visit gave residents and businesspeople alike the opportunity to demonstrate what the "capital" of Edwards County was like. Eugene Edwards offered the "spacious grounds" of his newly christened residence on Fourth Street, Trail's End, as a gathering place for "almost everyone in town."

The grounds were brightly illuminated with electric lighting until 10:30 p.m., when everyone was asked to retreat inside the Edwards residence for dancing. Members of the Kansas City Orchestra, who played on the lawn, eventually moved inside with the innumerable guests. Also, the Kansas City Glee Club was on hand for musical performances as well. Both the *Graphic* and *Mercury* recounted how Kansas City's most influential residents toured Kinsley, searching for its economic possibilities while bringing their own professional musicians. The *Kansas City Star* reported the day following the Kinsley visit that the delegates left Trail's End and went immediately to the White House for a meeting with President Roosevelt on economic matters. Kinsley's political position was rising, and therefore, so did its cultural output.

In the years to come, various community members joined together to create further large-scale musical productions on the stage at Flohr's Opera House, and they lived up to the building's name. In 1908, Kinsley's amateur musicians and actors staged Gilbert and Sullivan's comic opera *H.M.S. Pinafore*, featuring fifty local singers and a ten-piece orchestra. Charlie Edwards took a leading role as Sir Joseph Porter. He was joined by other familiar names in Kinsley's vibrant arts scene, including Nell Lewis Woods, Cora Lewis's sons Gilbert and Kelton, Lorin Raker and Ila Taylor's son Gus Hann, and the orchestra included Lester Beck on trumpet.

The *Graphic* and *Mercury* both set aside considerable space in their publications to celebrate the large production; the size and scope of the show were a prelude to what was to come with the Shakespeare festivals in future years. However, first, there was more comic opera: *The Chimes of Normandy*, billed as part of the "annual opera festival." Again, Charlie Edwards and Lorin Raker took large roles. This time, the production was larger than just Kinsley; Dodge City residents were also heavily involved, especially because it was directed by Bella M. Smith, who was from Dodge. Soon, Shakespeare replaced the comic opera phase, and one form of "high-brow" entertainment was superseded by the next.

Nevertheless, vocal music did not disappear; on the contrary, more music-centered forms of entertainment returned. Mabelle Wood Beeler, second wife to Charles William Beeler, a prominent local rancher, brought her years of vocal training to Kinsley to reorganize the Kinsley Ladies Chorus. She restructured the choir (where her sister-in-law, Gertrude Pearson Beeler, debuted as an accompanist in the 1897 *Dress Rehearsal*) in late 1914. The expressed purpose of the group was "for the betterment of the musical situation in Kinsley, and all proceeds [would] go to charity or the improvement of Kinsley or Edwards county." The group gave its first well-received concert in February 1915. The concert alone attracted seven hundred attendees, who were squeezed into the Methodist Church. Tickets sold for $0.25, and proceeds amounted to $140.

Mabelle Beeler led the ladies in rehearsals for the concert. She organized regular meetings where the members performed for one another and delivered talks on famous composers, musicians, vocalists and compositions. For the second annual concert, held in January 1916, the group, composed of twenty-four vocalists, appeared all dressed in white and were flanked by beautiful flowers and cages of canaries on both sides. This imaginative touch delighted the audience, as "the feathered songsters made themselves heard during the first half of the concert and grew less afraid and sang with great spirit during the remainder of the program." Again, the ladies performed for a capacity crowd of seven hundred, which filled the church's auditorium, the lecture room, the balconies, the choir seats and every other available foot of space. Florence Colver played violin pieces, and Lucile DeTar delivered memorable readings. The *Mercury* reported the event as "the greatest accomplishment in Kinsley musical history."

World events soon influenced the community's pursuit of music on the prairie. The Great War turned the third concert, held at the newly built Palace Theatre on November 13, 1917, into a benefit for the local chapter of the Red Cross. Organizers began the concert with Beethoven's words, "Music is a higher revelation than the whole of wisdom and whole of philosophy." The concert raised $150 for the Red Cross and was celebrated as an overall success.

Later that month, the Ladies Chorus made plans for the future and became the Ladies Chorus and Musical Club. This better represented the group's combination of singing with its educational programs of readings and recitals. It now had thirty-five members, and its programs often reflected the war in music and study topics, such as "Musical Atmosphere in the Soldiers' Camps and Abroad" and John Philip Sousa, "the band director, who is doing such wonderful work among the soldiers." Listening to records of the music under discussion played on the Victrola, the phonograph, added to the enjoyment. One meeting's discussion focused entirely on encouraging music in the youth "to make a town permanently musical" through the public schools. By 1919, the highly contagious influenza also required bans on community gatherings, including the Ladies Choir and Musical Club activities. Its next concert, still under the direction of Mabelle Beeler, was not held until March 1922 and featured twenty-two voices and a visiting concert pianist from Wichita.

The world was changing quickly in the 1920s, and music along with it. A December 21, 1922 editorial in the *Mercury* aimed to make Kinsley "a real center of interest" for musical performance. The article simultaneously warned of the "evils" of jazz and ragtime and implored readers to love the "right kind" of music. The era of opera festivals had passed, and despite the contrary arguments of its proponents, jazz was the beginning of a new musical future.

Nevertheless, throughout the decade, Kinsley's attention to musical performances of various kinds did not rapidly change with the nation's collective tastes; this became a sort of competition between Kansas communities. William Allen White congratulated his hometown of Emporia, Kansas, when one out of every eight people attended a recent "intellectual" play. Jim Lewis, editor of the *Graphic*, stated in a countering article that Kinsley, with a population of two thousand (by 1920), saw one in every three citizens attend this latest high-brow musical. In the following years, Kinsley's musical ensemble changed its name again, and for the last time, to simply the Kinsley Music Club. The group now focused on local music, as the art form evolved from jazz into new directions, not least of all rock-and-roll. The club remained active in supporting music in the community until 1959.

PIPE DREAMS: KINSLEY'S FIRST ORGAN

While the choir and music club brought concerts to the Methodist church, it was the majestic chords of a Reuter Organ that filled the sanctuary of the Kinsley Congregational Church. Community members organized Congregational Church in 1874, and it was the town's first church. When the congregation planned to move into its second building in 1886, the members wanted an organ. However, some people thought that the idea of Kinsley having an organ could only be a pipe dream. The town was on the frontier, and there were no organs west of Emporia.

Despite the obstacles, the congregation ordered a pipe organ from Henry Pilcher's Sons of Louisville, Kentucky. They planned to pay its $1,800 cost through donations and local fundraising. The Congregational Church saw that the new organ held the promise of the church hosting future concerts to raise the remaining money required, and it made the purchase. The community was very interested when the organ arrived and throughout its installation. It was big, occupying a space on the floor of ten and a half feet wide by seven feet deep and standing nearly twenty feet high. It was handsomely decorated in bright colors with gold and silver leaf and had 628 pipes and 12 stops. But what intrigued the people more was just how it worked, so on December 11, 1886, the *Mercury* explained it as a "marvel of ingenuity and somewhat difficult to describe" before listing the functionality of its mechanical components.

Professor Willis Peck was hired in early October as the first organist. He performed a dedication recital on December 15, 1886, which was "artistically and financially a complete success." The congregation sold tickets amounting to $450 to pay toward the outstanding balance on the organ. The *Mercury*'s report on the concert foreshadowed the Shakespeare festival's opening performance: "Mr. Peck seemed in his element as he took his seat at the organ, giving as the opening number the popular wedding march from Mendelssohn's 'Midsummer Night's Dream,' and in which he brought forth the power and beauties of the organ with fine effect." Peck was not the only guest to come in specifically to play the instrument. Henry Pilcher, owner of the organ company, traveled to Kinsley and played two numbers on the organ. That day, many talented local vocalists sang along with musicians who performed on the violin, cornet and piano.

During the ensuing years, the organ provided music for church services, weddings and concerts, some of which were performed by well-known organists, including Dwight Seymour of Colorado Springs. When he came in

The Henry Pilcher organ at the Congregational Church, decorated for the 1911 Edwards-Shouse wedding. *Edwards County Historical Society.*

1907 to repair the organ and perform a concert, he met Morton Schnatterly, who ran the local millinery shop with her sister, Myrton. A blossoming romance developed through their correspondence and visits when Dwight traveled through Kinsley on his way to perform in Kansas City or Morton made trips to visit friends in Colorado Springs. The community must have been slightly surprised when the forty-seven-year-old bachelor Dwight and forty-three-year-old spinster Morton married on September 11, 1909. Dwight was hired as the Congregational Church organist, and they settled down to live in Kinsley.

For the next two years, Dwight Seymour elevated the music scene in Kinsley. That fall, the *Graphic* hailed him as Kinsley's "leading musician who is one of the finest organists in the state." Unfortunately, the Seymours left Kinsley in 1911 when he was offered the organist position at the First Baptist Church in Topeka.

The Seymours' move made Dwight unavailable to play the organ for the social event of the century: the wedding of Marion Edwards, Charlie's sister,

Edwards-Shouse wedding, 1911. Eugene Edwards is at far left, Marion Edwards and Jouett Shouse are at center and Charlie and Lizzie Edwards are immediately at right. *Edwards County Historical Society.*

to Jouett Shouse (a future U.S. congressman and member of the Wilson administration) on October 19, 1911, in the Congregational Church. The organist from the Salina Cathedral was brought in to play for the ceremony, perhaps arriving on the same train that carried a carload of flowers and plants to decorate the church, organ and the Edwards mansion, Trail's End. Two thousand invitations were sent to the family's friends across all forty-six states, and 250 guests attended. For their convenience, a window of the mansion was replaced with a door that led out to the reception tent where an orchestra from Hutchinson played.

The Pilcher organ served the Kinsley congregation well until 1931, when a memorial gift allowed the congregation to purchase a "modern" and bigger organ from the Reuter Organ Company of Lawrence, Kansas. There is a silver lining in Kinsley's loss of such a beautiful old instrument:

the organ has now been completely restored and is the oldest church organ in Kansas today. Its majestic chords can be heard filling the sanctuary on Sunday mornings at the Methodist church in Cawker City, Kansas, 150 miles north of Kinsley.

KINSLEY MUSICIANS AND THEIR STORIES

While much of Kinsley's musical energy was generated by large groups of musicians performing together, individual performers gained a reputation by leading groups, performing solo concerts and writing their own music.

Lester Milton Beck (1876–1966) was born in Illinois, and later, he, his parents and his nine brothers and sisters settled in Offerle, Kansas. There Lester grew up farming with his father. Ultimately, despite having only an eighth-grade education, he influenced many lives in Kinsley through his love of music.

When Lester was a boy, the Santa Fe Railroad sent A.J. Hatch, a Wells Fargo express messenger, to Kinsley, where he settled down and married. Hatch was described in the May 9, 1889 issue of the *Mercury* as "a fine musician and under his skillful touch the grand old organ of which our Congregational friends are so proud, fairly talks to the audience." In 1891, Hatch opened a music store and a workroom in Kinsley to repair pianos and organs. He gave singing and music lessons and organized an orchestra. Orchestras at this time not only gave concerts but were also used for dances. More than likely, Hatch taught Lester Beck to sing and play the cornet, French horn and trombone. Around 1900, Lester moved into Kinsley and went to work as a salesman for Edwards, Noble & Company. Three years later, he joined Kinsley's coronet band under the direction of Hatch. He also met Lenna Evans, a talented young lady who shared his interest in music as she sang, played an instrument and participated in dramatic productions.

The *Graphic* reported a near disaster for Lester in its July 24, 1903 issue. After band practice one night, he had "slid his horn under the bandstand and walked home with a young lady" (probably Lenna). When he returned to pick up his instrument, he was shocked to discover that it had disappeared. A marshal located several alleged vagabonds with the horn making their way to the train depot. Apparently, the law enforcement officer was so "well-pleased at finding the tooter that he forgot to arrest them."

After many nights of walking home together after rehearsals and concerts, locals were not suprised when Lester and Lenna married in the Methodist parsonage on Sunday evening, May 6, 1906. However, the Beck marriage was not destined for happiness. Six years later, Lester filed for divorce, charging Lenna with "extreme cruelty and gross neglect of household duties, unwarranted jealousy and unreasonable requests with fits of crying and fainting which made life unbearable." The divorce was granted, and Lenna left Kinsley. Six months later, Lester took it upon himself to form the Kinsley Kid Band. Its twenty-six members were young men aged nine and up. Lester helped them pick out quality instruments, and the band gave its first public performance on December 7, 1912. After that, the name was changed to Beck's Boy Band.

The band grew to thirty-four members and was invited to perform at the 1913 Kansas State Fair. Beck recounted in the September 16 edition of the *Mercury*, "Everything seemed to go just right. The boys never did so well and I certainly was proud of them. They went through music without a slip that they had stumbled over at home." The article continued:

> *And the crowd, too, appreciated the work of the boys particularly and very naturally the smaller ones and a good many nickels and dimes found their way to the boys' pockets during the day. But this was not the only expression of appreciation received. Several times during the day enthusiastic women would grab one of the youngsters in their motherly arms and imprint a hearty kiss on a fair young face. The boys had a fine time and their work justifies our prediction a few weeks ago that they would bring honor to themselves and their town.*

The band continued its "honorable" performances and bolstered Kinsley's statewide reputation as an artistic capital. From 1912 to 1919, the ensemble's renown grew, playing concerts in parks, at churches, on Decoration Day and for social and club events throughout the area. With many events and the size of the ensemble, one can only muse at the impact Lester Beck had on the young men of Kinsley during the seven years the band performed.

Beck's Boy Band played its last concert in June 1919 for the Old Settlers Picnic. That month, Lester and his second wife moved to Dodge City, where they lived out their lives.

Cora Ellen Reed (1890–1952) was born in Marion, Kansas; she attended Kansas State Normal School, now Emporia State University, and taught public school for four years before marrying Hal Galbraith in 1909. Her husband was a telegrapher for the Missouri Pacific Railroad. The couple

Beck's Boy Band, circa 1913. *Edwards County Historical Society.*

Beck's Boy Band was but one band to perform in Kinsley; here, the Independent Order of the Oddfellows parades through town, April 1912. *Courtesy of Ed Carlson.*

lived in Aubry, Kansas, where they had one son, Jack. Cora divorced Hal in 1920, and four years later, she married Dr. Fred Dargatz.

Dr. Dargatz graduated in 1913 from the Universal Medical College in Kansas City and served in the medical corps in France during World War I. When his first wife died in 1918, he moved west. At the time of his marriage to Cora, Dr. Dargatz was practicing medicine in Macksville, Kansas, but they soon moved to Kinsley, where Dr. Dargatz established his office on the main street. The couple had no children, but Cora's son, Jack, lived with them until he graduated from Kinsley High School in 1929.

Cora quickly became part of Kinsley's vibrant cultural life. She helped reorganize the Kinsley Music Club, was a talented pianist and wrote and published poetry and song lyrics. Cora became Kinsley's second composer, after Ila Taylor, when she published the words and music for "Sugar Ain't Sweet Since I Kissed You" in 1927:

Sugar ain't sweet since I kissed you, that summer day,
Nobody knows how I miss you when you're away,
The birds seem so lonely, they sing for you only,
And I want you more than I can say.
Any place is heaven, when you smile at me,
Roses are red and violets blue,
but sugar ain't sweet ever since I kissed you,
And you gave to me your promise true, that summer day.

Around the time of Cora's publication, Nashville became a popular center for jazz bands and famous orchestras, despite the grumblings of detractors. Radio stations WSM and WLAC enticed musicians to come to Nashville to broadcast live music nationwide. Perhaps Cora began thinking about a career in Nashville and dreaming of her songs being performed at the Grand Ole Opry. This could have contributed to why she left both Kinsley and her husband in 1937 and went to Nashville.

Cora never returned to Kinsley, causing Dr. Dargatz to run out of patience and sue for divorce eight years later, claiming "extreme cruelty and gross neglect of duty." The divorce was granted one month before Dr. Dargatz died in November 1945. Cora died seven years later at age sixty-two in Bentonville, Arkansas, never realizing her dream of songwriting fame.

Josephine Hills (1879–1982) was born into a sheep-breeding family of means in Ohio. When her mother first seated her at the large, rosewood square piano for her first lessons, she was a very small child. Josephine attended a one-room schoolhouse where she played a small reed organ. Unable to reach the pedals when seated on the bench, she found it entirely natural to stand on the pedals to work them to play.

First, Josephine went to the Harcourt Place Seminary for Young Ladies and Girls preparatory school, where she excelled as a pianist. Her talent led one teacher to recommend that she study abroad. After she graduated and moved with her family to Kinsley in 1902, she did not forget that dream. She began teaching piano, but it was not long before she and the family realized that piano lessons alone might not generate the needed funds. Her father went to the bank and arranged a loan for her to study at the Royal Conservatory in Leipzig, Germany.

In 1905, Josephine, a classmate and her aunt, as a chaperone, sailed on the RMS *Carpathia* for Europe (the ship that would come to the aid of the *Titanic* seven years later). She reminisced about her year abroad in her later years, describing it as a "musical feast." She enjoyed many evening concerts, the opera and free rehearsal tickets to the Gewaird Hans Symphony Orchestra. Initially, she was under the famed concert pianist Alfred Reisenauer (himself a close pupil of virtuoso composer Franz Liszt). After her first lesson, Reisenauer praised some of her playing but, with "strong temperamental outbursts, condemned others." She requested a change of teachers, and from then on, she thrived under a different teacher. Before the year ended, the three ladies had seen many popular attractions across England, Italy, Switzerland, Austria and France. During the spring break, Josephine toured the home of Franz Liszt, her teacher's mentor, who had died twenty years earlier. She was thrilled when the housekeeper allowed her to play a few notes on Liszt's favorite piano.

Josephine Hills Boyd, circa 1930. *Kinsley Public Library*.

Josephine returned home to teach piano. Once back in Kinsley, she joined the group of poets and also played the Congregational Church organ. For her to practice, the custodian was hired to pump the organ for her for one hour every Saturday. He facetiously remarked, "Josephine Hills is no musician; she has to practice!" Her practice continued to pay dividends as reviews came in throughout the state after she performed at a Topeka concert upon her return. The *Topeka Capital* colorfully commented on September 22, 1905: "Surely all the smoldering fires of the ruby are contained in her playing." She continued to perform with "smoldering fire" alongside many of Kinsley's most talented people throughout the next decade by joining forces with artists of all types. For example, she often performed with Charlie Edwards in his theatrical programs.

In 1920, Josephine joined a concert company of Dorothy Merryman, one of Charlie's protégés, who had a fine contralto voice, and dancer Persis Colie. They gave eleven performances in Santa Fe Reading Rooms, entertainment facilities for the railroad's numerous employees, along the way to California. She wrote, "We were given the red-carpet treatment, were met at the trains, taken to the best rooms, and ate the fine meals for which the Harvey Houses were noted."

The following May, Josephine married Arthur Edwards (no relation to the Kinsley Edwards family), an English pianist and organist, and they made their home in Denver. But six months later, the bride became a widow when, in November, Arthur died suddenly of pneumonia. She returned to Kinsley to live with her mother and opened a piano studio on the second floor of a downtown business building. After her mother died in 1939, four years later, she married widower Robert Boyd. Josephine Hills Boyd died in 1982 at the age of 102, the oldest surviving artist from Kinsley's turn-of-the-century golden age.

Chapter 8

"Bohemian Gatherings"

Visual Arts, Fashion and Local Venues

In October 1916, the *Mercury* touted Kinsley's reputation: "Kinsley social life is unique among Kansas towns for the small Bohemian gatherings of its various art workers." This was not hyperbole or hometown bias; it was true and well known. Starting in Kinsley's earliest years, the performing arts were displayed, but so too were the fine arts. From arts festivals and fairs of the 1880s to the photography galleries and fashion shows of the 1920s, Kinsley celebrated all aspects of its cultural offerings. By the end of this golden age, the Palace Theatre was built and began showing films for the community, a role that it still fulfills more than a century after its opening.

Leah Williams Nolan: Doll Maker, Draftsman and Artist

Leah Williams (1906–1982) was five years old when her family moved to one of the last available claims in the sandhills, twelve miles southwest of Kinsley. She and her siblings spent their childhood riding horses and roaming the hills. In the spring of 1910, tragedy struck with the sudden death of her thirty-six-year-old mother from pneumonia. Leah recalled, "This was the end of thinking as a child, from now on I would have to be responsible for myself." It soon became too difficult for the saddened family to continue living at the homestead, so they moved into Kinsley.

Leah Nolan in Kinsley, circa 1918. *Kinsley Public Library*.

A bright, creative and popular student at Kinsley High School, Leah graduated as valedictorian in 1918. However, it was a challenging time. With World War I raging and the flu pandemic spreading, she received a scholarship and left Kinsley. She enrolled in secretarial classes at a business college in Lawrence, Kansas, and took on several jobs. One of Leah's three part-time gigs was in a large hardware store that sold art supplies where she enjoyed helping to arrange store displays.

Another health crisis struck the Williams family when Leah contracted tuberculosis. She spent over a year in rest and treatment at a state sanatorium. Her only complaint against the hospital was that the staff would not permit her to do anything. To help alleviate her boredom, she enrolled in a correspondence class in lettering. This class became the spark that set her on an art career. Leah recovered and moved in 1921 to Denver, where she enrolled in a course in poster art. She started making advertising placards and displays for store windows and theater lobbies.

Leah also began experimenting with constructing small papier-mâché figures for table favors, patterning them after people she saw. These small dolls had a wire armature covered with cotton and were wrapped in crepe paper. They were very detailed and intricate, right down to pinhead-sized fingernails, eyes and lips, all cut from crepe paper and glued on. Leah continued developing this technique and, by 1925, worked with photographers who used her figures in settings for cartoons and illustrations. The figures often depicted famous actors and were displayed in theaters in Denver—many performers, including famed comedian Fanny Brice, commissioned Leah for this purpose.

In 1924, Leah married William Nolan, but nine years later, she was divorced and living in Chicago. She continued making her figures for cartoon illustrations photographed for *Esquire* magazine, *Look* magazine and the *Saturday Evening Post*. World War II abruptly interrupted Leah's decision to study painting at the School of Design. Instead, in 1941, Leah took a three-month concentrated course in engineering drafting. She went to work for the military as a draftsman and then became a civilian engineer at the Palm Springs Army Air Force Base. After the war, she alternated her career in painting and exhibiting with commercial drafting.

Leah gave up drafting in 1967 and devoted her time to painting and exhibiting, often trying new ideas and techniques in her painting, figure construction and even video. Leah Williams Nolan returned to Kansas, where she died in Wichita in 1982 at the age of eighty. She is buried at Kinsley's Hillside Cemetery. One of her oil paintings hangs in the Kinsley Library, a 1973 gift from Leah to her childhood prairie home.

FRED EMERY WILSON: ARCHITECT AND ARTIST

Twelve years after his mother arrived in Kinsley in a covered wagon, Fred Wilson (1898–1978) was born. As a child, Fred showed talent in the arts like so many of his peers growing up in Kinsley's golden age. Early in his childhood, he won prizes at the Arts and Crafts Fair, and his theater interests manifested the summer after eighth grade when he and his brother Jerry appeared as two of the fairies of the celebrated 1912 *A Midsummer Night's Dream*. Fred participated in multiple facets of Kinsley's vibrant culture, joining Beck's Boy Band and then later the school band. In 1914, the latter ended its spring concert with band members acting in a one-act farce titled *The First Class Hotel*. Perhaps Fred was typecast as a jolly traveling salesman who made life miserable at the hotel by making fun of the food, breaking furniture and turning things upside down.

In high school, Fred never lost his love of a joke while remaining a good student. He served as the annual's assistant art editor and the athletic editor. The latter might account for the humorous individual pictures of the football team and their flattering captions despite their less-than-stellar record on the gridiron: "Fred was the quarterback on the 1916 team. He was a star in carrying the ball and tackling." During Fred's junior year, he played roles in *The New Co-Ed* and *What Would a Gentleman Do*. When Shakespeare's *The Comedy of Errors* was chosen for the senior class play, he was cast as one of the lead roles. This production, directed by Charlie Edwards, was the first time any class had decided to produce an unaltered Shakespeare play. Still, the selection was not a surprise after five years of the successful Shakespeare festival; the exuberance had not waned.

Fred was drafted into the army while attending Kansas State Agricultural College (now Kansas State University). World War I ended before he was sent overseas, so he completed his college education and earned his degree in architecture. He began his career in Tampa, Florida, until the stock market crash of 1929, when he was hired as an architect by the General Services Administration in Washington, D.C. He continued to paint portraits and landscapes there.

In 1930, Fred was questioned regarding a sensational D.C. murder investigation of Mary Baker. She was a young navy file clerk whose bloody body was found in a ditch of a remote section of Arlington National Cemetery on April 11. Fred and Mary had both worked in the Bureau of Aeronautics and had kept company with each other before his marriage to Betty Newman earlier that year. The day after Mary's body was found, Fred was questioned by both the D.C. and Arlington police. He admitted that he was to have met Mary at 5:00 p.m. on the night she was murdered, but she did not show up. After hours of interrogation, he was ruled out as a suspect and released. In the days and weeks to follow, the Capitol, Arlington County and Virginia State Police Departments, as well as navy and Department of Justice agents, all questioned another dozen men as suspects. Finally, a wealthy real estate man, Herman Campbell, was arrested and charged with the crime. During the trial in October, a new technology was used to microscopically compare the bullets from the crime to Campbell's gun. The comparison was found to be unreliable, and he was acquitted. The murder case was never solved.

Fred continued to work in D.C., and during World War II, when Fred was forty-three, he used his close connection with his college fraternity brother Milton Eisenhower (President Eisenhower's brother) to get back into the army to serve as an artilleryman. There he protected the U.S. coastline in California and Florida. When Fred retired to Florida, he devoted himself to painting likenesses and landscapes. Fred painted portraits of all the Edwards County Bank presidents, including his father, which are still on display at the Edwards County Museum.

DAVID A. LESTER: PIONEER ARTIST AND SCULPTOR

At Hillside Cemetery, just a mile northwest of Kinsley, there stands a monument dedicated to the Union soldiers and sailors of the Civil War. It was created in 1917 by David Lester, a Civil War veteran and a member of the Grand Army of the Republic (GAR). He was seventy-four years old when he fabricated the five figures and four bas-relief panels. Nearly a century passed before, in 1998, restoration efforts preserved it as an example of what is now called "grassroots art." One year later, scholar Randall Thies covered David's work in *Kansas History*:

> [He] *is best known as the creator of the Kinsley Civil War monument.... Although the monument was his greatest artistic accomplishment, Lester created many other works of art—mostly of a utilitarian nature—in his many years as a pioneer artist....Lester, and others like him, had a unique role in "civilizing" the west, adding beauty and refinement to the raw new storefronts and homes of frontier towns.*

Many Union veterans settled in Kansas, encouraged by the 1862 Homestead Act, which provided that any adult citizen who "had never borne arms against the US government" could claim 160 acres of surveyed government land. Although this was not a military service land grant, per se, as had been offered after the Revolutionary and 1812 wars, Union veterans could deduct the time they had served during the Civil War from the five-year residency requirement of the Homestead Act. Kansas soon became known as the "Great Soldier State," and it would come to have more GAR members per capita than any other state, with Post 241 as a thriving example.

David Lester, Civil War veteran and sculptor of Kinsley's Civil War monument, circa 1895. *Edwards County Historical Society.*

David Lester was one of the veterans who came to Kansas. He had been born on a farm near Schenectady, New York, on March 10, 1843. Shortly after the Civil War began in 1861, he enlisted in Company F of the Twenty-Seventh New York Volunteer Infantry. At the time, he was eighteen years old, and his records describe him as five feet, five inches tall, with a light complexion, black eyes and brown hair. He fought at Bull Run in the first major battle of the war, where his company lost 26 men and 44 wounded. The Twenty-Seventh New York Infantry engaged in many more battles, and 146 men were lost to fighting and disease.

There is no record of David ever suffering wounds or disease during his two years of service.

David was discharged in 1863 and returned to New York, where he would marry Eulalia Crannell ten years later; they had a son in 1877. The next year, the Lesters moved to Kinsley, where they would live and have two more children. David always described himself as an artist. He made his living painting and decorating houses and buildings. On July 31, 1891, he promoted his talents in an advertisement in the *Graphic*: "In this present age of progress the painter, paper-hanger and decorator is as necessary…to our well being as our tailor or house-furnisher, for he, with a skill and talent that belongs to his profession, makes a veritable Monte Christo palace out of what was chaos."

About this same time, he discovered photography and threw himself into that art. In the 1895 Kansas Census, he listed photography as his profession; he opened a gallery in a building behind Flohr's Opera House. David became proficient in producing bromide enlargements of pictures and photographs. Although none of his works has survived, his artistic talents also went beyond decorative works into true art. Kinsley chronicler Myrtle Richardson described David's studio in her book *The Great Next Year Country*:

> *School children who went to and from their classes by the studio were often fascinated with glimpses of the interior of the studio. They never opened the door, but should it be open as they were passing by, they were prone to step in and see what new picture was being produced on the easel. Frequently, there was nothing to be seen but globs of paint and messy rags. Over it all, the odor of turpentine and oil spoke for the activity of the owner of the studio.*

Sculptors crafted Civil War monuments in the East in the first twenty years following the war, but Kansas was busy settling the state, so it would take a few more decades before they appeared. However, from 1885 to 1917, the GAR inspired many communities to erect monuments, from simple obelisks to sentinel soldiers and real cannons.

In 1912, David joined GAR Post 241 and was the post commander by 1916. The post had considered building a monument for several years, and with artist David in command, it would finally come to be. He may have taken inspiration from an April 27, 1916 article in the *Mercury* describing Civil War veteran Samuel Perry Dinsmoor's large Garden of Eden environment in Lucas, Kansas. Not long after, he planned to build his monument out of reinforced concrete, much like Dinsmoor's figures.

Civil War monument by David Lester at Hillside Cemetery, circa 1917. *Kinsley Public Library.*

In November 1916, David Lester submitted a scale model for his design to Post 471. It was an ambitious project. Current evidence does not indicate that he had ever done anything in this technique or of this size before (an eight-foot-square base and reaching twenty-four feet tall). The model was displayed in the bank building, and the community was asked for input and support. The goal was to have it finished by Memorial Day, although whether it would be erected in Kinsley or at Hillside Cemetery was still undecided.

The following report, from the March 15, 1917 issue of the *Mercury*, offered a view of the monument's creation:

> *The first thing the visitor observes as he approaches the Lester studio, is a lifelike figure of an infantryman standing guard at the door.... One thing that impressed the inartistic reporter was the lack of much machinery or tools. Mr. Lester molds the concrete into the desired forms almost entirely with his hands.... He is doing the present work on a contract with local GAR post of which he is a member, and therefore is taking additional pride in the monument.*

David Lester completed the monument in two and a half months at a cost of $1,100, collected through donations. The decision was finally made to erect it atop the hill at the cemetery. Continued loyalty to the Union placed "Winged Victory" facing to the North, overlooking two soldiers' plots. Two of the bas-reliefs on the base, one of charging cavalry and one of four artillerymen with a field gun, both had their weapons pointing to the South.

The veterans were delighted with the monument and very proud when the community dedicated it on Memorial Day 1917. However, the United States' declaration of war the month before overshadowed the event. A few years after he completed the monument, David and his wife moved to Oklahoma City to be with their daughter. He died in 1927 at the age of eighty-four.

BEN ELY JR.: CARTOONIST AND PAINTER

Like Leah Nolan, eleven-year-old Ben Ely's (1897–1988) life was significantly transformed when the family moved from a rural Edwards County homestead into Kinsley in 1909. He would find his calling while attending Kinsley High School.

Ben Ely Jr. (1897–1988), circa 1916.
Kinsley Public Library.

It is a mystery where Ben and other would-be artists of Kinsley, like Fred Wilson and Leah Nolan, received any early art training. The visual arts were mentioned in school, but there was no time in the crowded curriculum for classes. In 1901, a Council of Supervisors of the Manual Arts was organized to advance the manual arts of drawing, design and constructive work in public schools. Potentially, this encouraged Kinsley's domestic science and manual training teachers to integrate art into their classes. Every year, the Woman's Club exhibited works put together by their federation or by the Roullier Art Galleries of Chicago, much like the Arts and Craft Fairs of the early years. Teachers were encouraged to discuss the paintings, pottery and other art with their students. David Lester's studio was across from the school, and the children liked visiting. Perhaps he offered guidance. Also, correspondent courses were available; students could have learned from books and then honed their natural talent.

Regardless of how Ben learned, he was already recognized for his artistic talent as a junior in high school. He gave chalk talks for literary programs and was on the Kinsley High School annual staff, becoming the art editor his senior year. His cartoons and drawings appeared on many pages of the yearbooks from 1914 through 1917. He used the black-and-white ink illustrations in the popular art nouveau style of the day. The yearbooks reveal that Ben was active in clubs and sports and acted and worked on sets for the theatricals. Around the school, Ben was "known by his neckties." As a senior, he earned the following limerick in the annual:

There is a young man we call Ben
Who always makes use of his pen.
If you'll take time to look,
At the cartoons in this book.
You'll say he is great among men.

That summer after Ben graduated, Charlie Edwards produced Shakespeare's *Twelfth Night*, and Ben worked on the scenery. With his good friends, brothers Jerry and Fred Wilson and Tom Mairs, he participated in many of the theatrical productions. Ben returned to Kinsley for several years during the summers to continue acting and designing scenery for plays. Many of these productions were held at the new Palace Theatre. He also

Opposite: Ben Ely's yearbook art nouveau drawing depicting the theatrical character Pierrot, who had appeared frequently on local stages, serenading his love interest, 1916. *Kinsley Public Library.*

Right: Ben Ely sketch for a poem by Kinsley poet laureate Nell Lewis Woods, circa 1934. *Kinsley Public Library.*

exhibited his work at Tom Mairs's art and photography gallery. In 1927, Ben began working for the Newspaper Enterprise Association in Cleveland. His illustrations appeared in many papers, including the *Hutchinson News*. Ben wrote, "My first story was for the weekly issue, a Wild West Thriller, called 'The Aztec Mystery.'"

By 1935, Ben was married and working as an illustrator in New York City. That year, he painted seventeen richly colored portraits to illustrate a large book titled *Famous Indian Chiefs* for Whitman Publishing Company. Each page contained a short biography of the Native American leaders, including Crazy Horse, Tecumseh, Geronimo, Sitting Bull and thirteen others. The next year, he created and illustrated a regular children's column in the *Country Home Magazine* called "Agri and the Magic Corn Silk." In the 1940s, the Elys moved to Colorado, where he continued to paint, exhibit his watercolors and portraits and judge art competitions. Ben died in 1988, just two months after his wife died. They are buried in Lander, Wyoming.

"I Am Here to Stay": Photographers in Kinsley and Edwards County

In Kinsley's most formative days, there was little difference between a photographer and any other type of visual artist. By September 1890, there had been seventeen years of relatively itinerant photographic artists or no photographers at all, so very few people expected that a twenty-one-year-old woman would do what at least seven previous men had failed to do: make a living as a photographer.

Alma Ditus (1869–1957), the eldest child of a recently deceased Civil War veteran, had come to Kinsley from Larned to see how she could support her widowed mother and six younger siblings. The one job Kinsley needed and had always respected was a photographer. However, it was one of many careers that women were generally discouraged from doing at the time. Undaunted, Alma arrived in March and purchased Daniel Atkins's gallery; she got to work immediately. Alma took her equipment around town and photographed locales with the people in them. For two years, she worked diligently and effectively, producing many prints and cabinet photos (several of which remain today and can be viewed at the Edwards County Historical Museum). Only after this did she announce, "I am here to stay," a statement already lived up to, as at that point she had been there longer than her forerunners.

Alma Ditus's artistic success in Kinsley continued. By May 1896, Alma was in her sixth year in the photography business, and to keep her work stable, she teamed up with a business partner under the company Nelson & Ditus Art Gallery. However, while the business's books were stable, the old building the studio resided in, constructed by Michael Brumfield ten years earlier, was not as sound. The *Mercury* reported on May 14, 1896, that it was "gradually settling to the west, and unless speedy attention is paid it will collapse." Alma Ditus took this as a sign to leave town and move her business to Topeka; she had supported her mother through her six years as a professional photographer so that her siblings could enter the workforce. Now she could move on with her own life. After living in Topeka for twenty years, her first husband died, and she moved to Long Beach, California, and remarried. As a testament to her lifelong undaunted spirit, she gave birth to her only child at age fifty-one in 1920.

Elsewhere in Edwards County, beginning around 1907, Winfred Orlando Durstine (1869–1947) began photographing Belpre's people, buildings, community life and the nearby towns of Fellsburg and Trousdale. When

Left: Alma Ditus, Kinsley-based photographer, circa 1893. *Edwards County Historical Society*.

Below: Winfred Orlando Durstine with his photography wagon, circa 1910. *Edwards County Historical Society.*

a fire destroyed much of the town of Belpre in 1907, Durstine's studio burned down. His resourceful solution was to outfit his studio in a car that could be pulled around the area by a team of horses. Besides having a portrait studio within it, this photo car on wheels took him to schools, ball games, country homes and the wheat fields. According to Myrtle Richardson in *The Great Next Year Country*, clients often tired of trying to hit a suitable pose for Durstine. But he would keep trying until "he wearied the toughest subject, and he usually came up with an excellent picture for the effort."

It appears that Durstine had difficulty earning a living just through his photography. Over the years, he taught school, served as justice of the peace and was a police judge. His respectable penmanship landed him a clerk job assisting the county probate judge. Through it all, he kept taking pictures, especially outdoors. In 1919, the *Mercury* reported that "Belpre has a real artist for a citizen and a town booster, for he [Durstine] can put up just as strong a talk for the old hometown as he can for portraits and general photograph work."

Durstine lived a long life, but not without controversy and seldom with money. He died in 1947 and was buried in an unmarked grave in the potter's field at Hillside Cemetery. However, his story and the subjects he captured in his images continue to live on. In 2015, more than six hundred glass negatives were rescued from the landfill and given to the Edwards County Historical Society featuring the photographic work of Winfred Orlando Durstine. Subsequently, these extraordinary photos were digitized by the Kansas Historical Society.

Meanwhile, in Kinsley, during Durstine's time, photographer John Cox was preparing to turn the keys of his studio over to an artistic Renaissance man: an actor, director, musician, dancer, painter, photographer, fashion designer and erstwhile machine-gunner, Tom Mairs.

TOM MAIRS: KINSLEY IN NEW YORK AND NEW YORK IN KINSLEY

Born in Milan, Missouri, to Bob and Esther Sterling Mairs, Tom Mairs (1895–1968) arrived in Kinsley at the age of ten when his father bought one of Eugene Edwards's properties. Tommy, as he was known then, immediately felt at home in the town's extensive arts and cultural environment, winning annual prizes for his visual artwork. He graduated from Kinsley High

School in 1914 and went to work at age sixteen, filling in as a soda jerk at the A&A Drug Store. Soon, Tom also began piano lessons and learned the era's "aesthetic dancing" (essentially a variety of European folk dances), which he put into practice in the 1916 production of Shakespeare's *Twelfth Night*. Throughout this era, he participated in community-based theater productions, such as the Shakespeare festivals and the Kinsley High School productions. His friend Lorin Raker had left for New York City years earlier to excel in a professional acting career, and Tom observed his success, waiting for his own opportunities.

Out of high school for four years, Tom had since tried his hand at being a soda jerk, a drugstore clerk and a photography assistant with John Cox, but none of these jobs seemed to move him closer to the success that Lorin had attained. At one point, Tom attempted a semester at the University of Kansas, but none of these options seemed right. As an artist with many interests, most of his favorite activities could only materialize in his free time. Tom certainly admired Charlie Edwards, who had served as a mentor, so when the opportunity arose in March 1917, he followed him to Kansas City and performed with a new theater company theater, the Harlequin Players.

From working with his mentor's many sources of inspiration, Tom could learn more than a semester studying literature at any university. During this time, he served as Charlie's lead protégé. However, since that role did not earn an income, he entered the employ of Charlie's father, Eugene Edwards, as his personal chauffeur and served as an "advance man" for the theater company. He hoped that he would not have to linger in either of these jobs as he waited for word on an application to attend school in New York City.

In the fall of 1917, Tom received the good news. He was accepted into the School of Fine and Applied Arts in New York, and he soon triumphantly departed, ready to be the next Charlie Edwards, Lorin Raker or Gilmor Brown. In the nation's largest city, Tom saw the latest fashion, the best theater and the most remarkable turns in the arts. For a twenty-two-year-old born and raised in rural America, the culture shock to early twentieth-century city life must have been pronounced. Most of all, it was not an easy time to study arts and culture, as other young men his age suited up for the trenches and went to war.

Despite the bustling allure of New York City and its cultural scenes, Tom had to make the difficult choice to return to Kinsley; he did not graduate. He reluctantly went to work at the Trail Drug Store but was too discontented

Thomas James Mairs (1895–1968), Kinsley High School yearbook, 1915, *Kinsley Public Library.*

to stay long. Tom enlisted, entering the Naval Academy at Annapolis, Maryland. He became one of the first graduates to specialize in the machine gun. After months of specialized work, he became an instructor and taught squads of new recruits how to utilize one of the newest and deadliest weapons of war. His skills in instruction kept him safely off the front lines, and by April 1919, he had been discharged.

After trying his hand at an art designer job in Kansas City for the Burnap Paper House throughout the rest of 1919, Tom returned home to Kinsley and accepted a job at his brother's pharmacy, Goddard and Mairs. But it was not long before he hopped to his next job as a clerk at the Farmers and Merchants State Bank of Kinsley.

As Tom bounced between moneymaking careers, he continued with the arts scene, and it slowly started to pay off. By November 1920, he had been promoted to drama director of Kinsley's High School's plays, filling the shoes of his mentor, Charlie Edwards, which had been empty for some time. Tom went on to direct *Peg o' My Heart* (1920), *Fannie and the Servant Problem* (1921) and *Mrs. Bumstead Leigh* (1922) with local high school students, all of which were produced at the Palace Theatre. In 1921, he also organized and directed a production of *Her Husband's Wife*, held at the Palace Theatre. This production featured the triumphant return of Kinsley luminary Lucile DeTar Colyer, who had just finished a professional engagement with a New York–based performance company. She was yet another of Tom's contemporaries who blazed the unlikely path of professional success.

Tom announced that the play, featuring Lucile, was to be part of Kinsley's "annual summer play festival," an idea that had disappeared after 1916's *Twelfth Night.* He planned to continue the grand festival that granted Kinsley so much fame in the previous decade. While Tom was undeniably talented and artistic, the festival required much more than vision. It necessitated large amounts of financial and community support and, most of all, unbounded enthusiasm. Maybe he was missing one of these ingredients, or perhaps the pre-war civic patriotism of the 1910s was a far cry from the rambunctious discontent of the Jazz Age. Whatever the reason, the Arkansas Valley Dramatic Festival could not be resurrected.

Unable to revive the once-in-a-lifetime energy of the 1910s, Tom decided to embrace another area of art that interested him (something he was exposed to in New York City), one that had just started to emerge in the previous decade: the fashion show. The community was unsure of how it felt about a relatively metropolitan display as part of the long-running theater tradition. The *Graphic* reiterated those concerns: "It was feared by many that Director Tom Mairs had taken on something beyond the power of local talent, despite the fact that Kinsley is known to be lavish in its wealth of ability along the lines of Thespian art." Tom overcame these doubts and closed his *Mrs. Bumstead Leigh* production at the Palace Theatre with a fashion show. He coordinated with local businesses and used his love of fashion to help them sell their products. To draw people into the styles presented on his "runway," Tom recruited Kinsley's poet laureate, Nell Lewis Woods, to write "rhymes full of clever ideas well told." Many styles appeared on the runway, including golf goods, men's and ladies' ready-to-wear, Jackie Coogan suits, shoes, hosiery, silks, evening apparel and even watches. Tom's unexpected idea worked well, earned praise in the papers, and it helped to launch his next project. He soon took over the photography studio of John Cox, his former boss.

Now with his own studio and business to maintain, Tom had to step back from directing educational theater. The *Graphic* noted that Tom is "naturally of an artistic temperament," which combined well with his "kindliness, helpfulness and ability." His friends felt sure that he could find both personal satisfaction and success in his next occupation as a professional photographer and artist. Before he could settle into his job, the Kinsley Chamber of Commerce asked him to conduct yet another fashion exhibition less than two months after Kinsley's debut show.

Never one to miss an opportunity, Tom agreed and joined a group assembling an indoor circus and carnival to celebrate the opening of a large garage at 302 Sixth Street in the town center. However, it was much more challenging to assemble the show in the chaos of an indoor garage-circus (Kinsley always relished a circus) than within the comfortable confines of the Palace Theatre. While the garage was large, perhaps Stanley Earp, the building's owner, and the other organizers were too zealous about how much one space could accommodate, causing difficulties for Tom. On June 15, 1922, the *Mercury* detailed the literal circus that awaited Kinsley. In addition to the fashion show, which received top billing, it included live alligators,

Nell Lewis Woods (*front*) in costume for one of her characters, potentially Miora, Queen of the Fortune Tellers, circa 1922. *Kinsley Public Library.*

Miora ("Queen of the Fortune Tellers," played by "none other than Mrs. Nell Lewis Woods, who is ever ready to assist any worthy cause"), boxing, wrestling, carnival stands, sleight of hand performers, confetti booths, boisterous "calithumpian" artists and musicians. Finally, two more aspects were "turned over to Tom to look after," two attractions that certainly were popular: the "Bathing Beauties and Hula Dancers." It was a nostalgic revival of 1880s traveling performers.

The chamber of commerce publicly thanked Tom for his efforts as it carefully acknowledged that he could not stage the fashion show "as extensively or as thoroughly" since the venue lacked "ample" space. Of course, one can read between the lines that Tom Mairs was not pleased that his fashion show had devolved into a toasty garage (in June) filled with live alligators, wrestlers, boxers and confetti. Hopefully he acknowledged that the event was far more unique than anything dreamed up by his friends in New York.

Meanwhile, if Nell's fortuning-telling Miora could predict the near future of the evening's host, Stanley Earp, or the building they all reveled in, Kinsley would be stunned at what was to come. Earp had a large, relatively secret basement installed in the building with a ramp leading outside. Through this ramp, he hid and eventually sold stolen automobiles in a theft ring. He and his associates stole at least ninety cars for fifteen months following the opening carnival. Fortunately for Tom Mairs, with this future in store, the carnival-circus-fashion show was not destined to be an annual event.

With the garage hullabaloo behind him, Tom worked on advertising his studio. He continued to partner with the chamber of commerce to produce events and promote his business, leading to his directing a one-act play, *Bills*, in November. Tom's good friend, artist Ben Ely, produced the stage scenery. The *Mercury* celebrated the work, stating that he "never does anything by halves" before calling him "our invincible Tom Mairs." However, despite his profession, Tom had not left behind his days as a machine gun instructor at the Naval Academy. He joined with fifteen other men on October 24, 1922, to form the Kinsley Rifle Club and submit their materials to the National Rifle Association while also searching for a "suitable rifle range."

Contrary to the confidence displayed in the local papers and by his family and friends, Tom did not feel "invincible," as his photography business was not highly profitable. His varied hobbies did not pay the bills, from the rifle club to fashion shows. Searching for options, he began to host art from his other artist friends like Ben Ely in his galleries and promote game nights and events to bring people in.

However, the springtime brought a distraction from these business endeavors when his friend and mentor Charlie Edwards floated back into town from his dalliances at the Algonquin Round Table in New York and offered him a significant role on his production team. May 1923 marked the fifteenth year since Charlie and Tom had first participated in a Kinsley play together. And now, Charlie billed Tom as his assistant director—the second time in nearly three decades he selected anyone for that role. Considering the pair's long working relationship and that Tom had been producing in town constantly during his absence, the choice was obvious; he was the heir apparent to Kinsley's theatrical renown.

The directing duo selected and collaborated on the recent Broadway success *Three Live Ghosts* and established their headquarters as the Mairs Studio, the same building that hosted all Kinsley's photography needs since 1898. However, this project did not focus on that aspect of Tom's skill. To bring the play to life on stage at the Palace Theatre, Charlie and Tom assembled a cast of about twenty local players and went to work. Ever reliable, the local press began the fanfare refrain for Charlie's first homecoming in three years. On June 7, 1923, one fan going by the initials "MAW" wrote a poem published in the *Mercury* that celebrated the local actors and Kinsley's theatrical legacy. The writer ended by acknowledging that the incredible atmosphere in Kinsley for literature, drama, music and art was meant for the "pages of history":

OUR HOME TOWN PLAYERS
We're proud of our home talent
New York has nothing on us!
When we want a high class production
Kinsley gives it without any fuss

We're only a town of two-thousand
But Charles Edwards, he's been on Broadway!
He's sat in the glare of the foot-lights
He knows the talent to play!

He's found it before in Kinsley
And these will not be the last!
'Tis written on the Pages of History
Come to Kinsley to get your cast!

Comparisons to New York were irresistible, and Tom's next production was more than just a restaging of a popular Broadway show. He added his own stamp to the *Three Live Ghosts* with his "second annual fashion show," which undoubtedly redeemed the crocodile-infested garage-circus fashion show of yesteryear. Tom and Charlie secured press coverage in papers from Dodge City to Wichita, and Tom received credit for "originating" the "popular entertainment" in Edwards County.

Meanwhile, in another example of how all aspects of the arts frequently interacted, Charlie and Nell Woods wrote self-proclaimed "doggerel" verses to accompany the fashion display. These mini-narrative poems provided a story of "Kinsley in New York," highlighting the various fashion options made locally available by merchants, featuring more than "fifty brilliantly dressed models." The premise behind the fashion show is that two characters attending school in New York City meet together and reminisce on "incidents back in the old hometown." Then models strutted across the stage with each reminiscence, displaying a merchant's outfit. Again Charlie and Tom emphasized metropolitan connections, specifically where the rights to produce the play came from (New York City) in their press releases.

When *Three Live Ghosts* and the Second Annual Fashion Show premiered, the Palace Theatre was at capacity, and the *Mercury* described the event as a "riot of color and beauty." They took the show on the road to Stafford for their Memorial Day activities. However, the events were bittersweet, and the creative team went their separate ways. Again, Charlie could feel his pocket watch ticking. He had to fulfill his firmly established routine of returning to his professional work in New York, Kansas City or Massachusetts.

Around the same time, Tom's lease on the photography studio expired, and "Kinsley's most proficient artist" had a choice: would he try to continue his business or search for something more stable? The photography income was not steady enough, or maybe he simply spent too much time organizing theater and fashion to focus on it. To make matters more difficult, John Cox, now the town's previous successful photographer, had returned. As was evident from the earliest years, Kinsley was not big enough for two full-time photographers. Moreover, theatrical and fashion show directors were not viable occupational options in small-town America.

By the end of 1923, Tom made a difficult decision to defer his dreams of art, theater and performance and enter the pharmacy business with his brother, Chester. He did not inherit and take charge of the summer festival. The two brothers purchased a building in Pratt and opened the Mairs Pharmacy. Tom remained in this business for three years, occasionally returning to Kinsley to see theater productions. But those productions, too, were slowing in number. Tom's brother married, and it must have seemed like everyone's lives were moving forward but his.

In April 1926, the *Mercury* reported that Tom had "severed" his connection with his brother. The signs in the train depots and elsewhere that had always pointed toward New York City never pointed back to Kinsley. And likewise, Tom did not look back. Maybe he heard the rumors from his Kinsley friends that Charlie was trying to restart the great Shakespeare festival. That did not come to pass either, and this era ended when he learned of the sudden and tragic death of his close friend and mentor six weeks later; he could not leave his new home to make it back for the Kansas City funeral.

When he arrived in New York, Tom worked as a clerk, first for the Pennsylvania Railroad and then for the U.S. Army. He lived there for forty-two years; he never married, and his theatrical and artistic contributions after moving to New York City remain unclear. Tom died at his sister's home in Oklahoma City in 1968 at the age of seventy-two. Tom wrestled with the duality of urban versus rural life, as did Charlie. They both used New York to promote his productions in Kinsley while implicitly embracing the line from the promotional poem, "We're proud of our home talent, New York has nothing on us!"

His personal history—from background character to lead actor and then becoming a director, photographer, local fashion champion and machine gun instructor—reminds us of the victories and struggles, then and now, of making a career as an artist in small-town America and beyond. As he came of age, his life was entwined with Kinsley's artistic heritage. But when the world radically changed in the 1920s, and the emphasis no longer remained on Kinsley's collective accomplishments but rather on its comparison to New York, many of the performing artists felt that they needed to be elsewhere. Perhaps Tom's sentiment was not so different than that of his friend and mentor Charlie, who wrote from his metropolitan job in one of his final poems: "Dear God, my home is fair and dear/I'd like to be both there and here!"

THE PALACE THEATRE

Kinsley entered the silent film era in 1912 when William Harwood established the first moving picture house in town, the Palace Theatre, within the newly constructed Marsh and Bidwell building on Main Street. Locals were happy to have this new entertainment. However, there were some nerves; theaters were notorious for starting fires in town, a devastating threat the old-timers could still remember. Adding hot projectors and highly combustible film to gas lighting and flammable curtains only increased the risk. To eliminate this hazard, Harwood placed the projector outside of the building. The two-hundred-seat theater opened in April and began showing the new three-reel feature films and newsreels, besides hosting live plays, performances and concerts. The silent films of the day were far from silent and not complete without musical accompaniment. Managers hired talented local pianists like Josephine Hills to play scores that added excitement, suspense and romance to these films.

In 1917, local dentist Dr. Charles Sterrett (1873–1940), Dr. James Donnell and Wilbur Broadie opened the competing Community Theatre across the street and just one block east of the Palace. They advertised the amenities of their theater as "a gold-fiber daylight screen, the best made, and the machine will be of the same make as that used for the showing of 'Snow White,' in Convention Hall at Kansas City." This new projecting machine ran on direct current, which claimed to eliminate the flickering images.

At this same time, Harwood began constructing a new Palace Theatre a few doors east of the old Palace on the prominent intersection of Sixth Street and Niles Avenue because the other theaters were too small. When it opened on July 10, 1917, the community celebrated it as one of Kansas's finest, most complete, artistic playhouses. Not since the construction of Flohr's Opera

The Palace Theatre, circa 1985. *Courtesy of William Reah.*

House in the mid-1880s did an enterprising community member assemble a venue with the sole purpose of entertainment. The *Graphic* reported that on its opening night, the Palace "was overflowing," with nearly all of Kinsley's artists in attendance, leaving many patrons standing. Its large, lighted marquee proclaimed that it truly was a palace. The following year after opening, Harwood sold the Palace to Sterrett. After running both the Palace and the Community Theater for a short time, Sterrett closed the latter.

This building far surpassed any previous facility in town. Four hundred people could be seated in the auditorium and one hundred on the balcony. It was equipped with a proscenium stage for the actors, dressing rooms and basement entries into the orchestra pit (a manager later removed the last two features to enlarge the stage); also, the architect thoroughly prepared it for cinema. The Palace boasted wide aisles, with room between the seats equipped with a wire hat rack at the bottom of each fold-down seat. The high ceiling accommodated a flyway for large flats of scenery. In 1925, a large fire screen, hand-painted with a classic Arabian scene, was installed. It still hangs in pristine condition behind the proscenium arch. The fire screen was ready to be dropped to cut off the audience from a fire on the stage or to isolate a fire in the auditorium from reaching the stage. Fortunately, it never had to be used. Meanwhile, for projector safety, the architect housed it on the balcony in a room with a concrete floor, metal walls covered with concrete and a fireproof door, making the room as nearly fireproof as possible. If the hot bulb of the projector or the combustible film caught fire, someone could shut off the room from both the audience seating and the stage.

The Palace Theatre's long and narrow shape characterizes this configuration, a popular architectural style for theaters in the early twentieth century called the "shoebox" design. The building measures 120 feet long by 33 feet wide and has a high ceiling, which provides ideal acoustics. As for the stage, it is 20 feet deep, and in 1917, it already had a large switchboard, giving "opportunity for many different lighting effects."

The Palace hosted motion pictures starring the famous actors of the day. Various groups staged plays there, including Kinsley High School class productions, plays produced by Charlie Edwards, Tom Mairs and traveling troupes. The Palace also hosted famous touring speakers and performers. One of the country's most celebrated orators, William Jennings Bryan (three-time Democratic nominee for president of the United States), spoke at the Palace on March 21, 1918. Countless concerts, events and speeches were held on the Palace's stage too. It was a vibrant and active community hub.

On September 12, 1929, headlines for a *Graphic* article read, "Talkies Are On in Big Town Fashion at the Palace–Large Out-of-Town Crowds Expected to Attend Talking Feature Shown Here—Sound Is Almost Perfect." After a two-year wait, talking motion pictures had finally arrived in Kinsley, marking a shift from silent films to the new era of the spoken word. In preparation, Dr. Sterrett had renovated the Palace with a quieter cooling system and padded the walls with felt to dampen echoes. He also had equipment installed to play the Vitaphone large wax sound discs. However, the discs were not perfect. Spliced film no longer synchronized with the sound, and the needle often jumped grooves in the middle of a speech or song. Despite these technical challenges, introducing "talkies" at the Palace Theatre was a noteworthy event that shaped the coming century of entertainment.

Since those renovations, the Palace has continued to reflect changes in the movie theater business. The Sterrett family ran the theater until 1958, after which it had several owners. Movie sound was transferred to the film. Next, film went from black-and-white to color and 3-D; eventually, the industry replaced film with digital technology. The Palace remained open through all of the accompanying equipment changes and major remodeling again in 1950.

In 1999, the nonprofit Palace Theatre Association took over the theater. Through its dedication, it was placed in the National Register of Historic Places in 2005. With funding and volunteers coming from the community and the E-Team (Entertainment Team), current movies are still being shown every weekend. Today, more than a century after its construction, the Palace Theatre is one of Kansas's few remaining "shoebox" design theaters. It remains a place where generations of people from Edwards County gather for entertainment while recognizing a long history of arts and culture in Kinsley.

Epilogue

The arrival of the twentieth century brought seismic social and technological change. Some ideas faded while others grew; however, the railroad that built the town maintained its place at the center of daily life, culture and business. Nevertheless, the vision that Kinsley could become the next metropolis through a series of "boom years" vanished along with the various sugar mills that held the hopes of yesteryear's prospectors. Many still believed, however, that Edwards County could be a community destined for great cultural achievements. A new generation, the first one raised in Kinsley—composed of artists, theater-makers and musicians—proved these lofty goals. Inspired by women like Cora Lewis, Lizzie Edwards and Alma Ditus, this generation, now in their twenties, grew up on a steady diet of community-based cultural clubs and live performances.

The early to mid-1910s were the height of Kinsley's golden age of arts, cultural activity and entertainment. The *Hutchinson Gazette* wrote that people traveled from Kansas City and St. Louis to attend performances and that "all roads led to Kinsley." Edwards County teemed with the humanities from opera to Shakespeare and original poetry to musical compositions. The January 27, 1916 edition of the *Mercury* proclaimed, "Kinsley Girls Win Remarkable Distinction," before describing that Lucile DeTar, Persis Colie and others had been selected to go on a performance tour of the Santa Fe Railway, from Chicago to San Francisco and back again.

The railroad superintendent of "Reading Rooms," Samuel Edwin Busser, Kinsley's onetime pastor, chose Lucile DeTar and her company for this gig.

The Kinsley Depot for the Santa Fe Railroad, circa 1905. *Edwards County Historical Society.*

Busser led efforts to improve "conditions of railroad employees" in 1898. When he inaugurated this new role for the Atchison, Topeka and Santa Fe Railroad, he mirrored the cultural work done in Kinsley to banish the Wild West and bring in refinement and art. Busser outlined his motto to the forty thousand railroad employees in a handbook: "Give a man a bath, a book and entertainment that appeals to his mind and hopes by music and knowledge, and as he becomes more faithful to himself he is more valuable to the company." Of all the places Busser had ever served during his time in the ministry as both a pastor and a bishop, something about Kinsley lodged in his heart. After Lucile DeTar and her associates performed, Superintendent Busser wrote to Kinsley's unofficial statesman, Eugene Edwards, who then shared it with the *Mercury*:

> *They are one of the best companies we have ever had....I am proud of them because they are from Kinsley....They gave it with such force and threw their hearts into it so that our employees went wild over Kinsley.*

In his letter, Busser also passed along the announcement posted in stations all along the line. The railroad brought a small settlement to life on the short grass prairie, and now that small town gave back to the railroad in a spectacular way:

> *Probably nowhere in the great state of Kansas is there greater musical and dramatic talent than in the thriving city of Kinsley, the capital city of Edwards County. To get the best along any of the lines of art, one needs not spend many hours in finding it....* [Miss DeTar's company] *will give a most remarkable program and it will clearly indicate to our employees that Kinsley is not very far from Boston.*

Thirty years earlier, Busser entertained snowbound Bostonians in Kinsley and proved to them the remote town's worth. Now, after decades of work to edify people across the span of the sprawling railroad system, the man who eulogized Mayor John Marsh after his tragic murder triumphantly announced undeniable progress. While Busser's onetime home was not a metropolitan city like Boston, its citizens had developed and refined all of the cultural offerings of one. For one more decade to come, "all roads" led to Kinsley.

KINSLEY'S GOLDEN AGE: A LASTING IMPACT

Charlie Edwards and his team of creatives significantly contributed to Kinsley's golden age of the arts during the first quarter of the twentieth century. However, Charlie's work, theatrical and poetic, inspired many people from Western Kansas to New York and from Massachusetts back to Oklahoma as well. Three of the five performers featured in this concluding section graduated from Kinsley High School and learned directly from Charlie. Their professional success can be traced back to unlikely theatrical performances in Kinsley, Kansas.

Lorin Raker (1891–1959) was Kinsley's homegrown professional actor and a member of the first generation of film stars. Born in Joplin, Missouri, he moved with his family to Kansas as a young boy around the turn of the century. Lorin was one of Charlie's earliest protégés, studying drama and serving as a reporter for the *Mercury*. He left town the year before the Arkansas Valley Dramatic Festival's inaugural performance to begin his career with professional theater companies elsewhere in Kansas. In the 1910s, he became involved in the film industry, working with Universal Studios in various filming locales worldwide, of which many of these films are now lost. In 1919, he had his breakout role in Émile Chautard's *The Mystery of the Yellow Room* before returning to Broadway throughout the early 1920s. Lorin then went to Los Angeles, where he formed his own company and occasionally teamed up with Gilmor Brown, a man he first saw perform in Kinsley more than two decades earlier. After playing a few leads for Gilmor in the early '30s, he directed *Smoke Screen* at the Pasadena Community Playhouse in June 1935. By the end of his life, he had worked on more than one hundred film and TV gigs, many of which were uncredited, like his role in the classic 1947 film *Miracle on 34th Street*.

Lorin's occasional collaborator, Gilmor Brown (1886–1960), is known for his forty-three-year tenure with the Pasadena Playhouse as the founding artistic director. By the end of his life, he had created what famed British dramatist George Bernard Shaw called the "Athens of the West." At his world-renowned theater, Gilmor premiered original work by America's first generation of homegrown playwrights and authors, including Eugene O'Neill, Tennessee Williams, F. Scott Fitzgerald and Percy MacKaye. He went from an itinerant actor roaming the Kansas prairies to a theatrical titan. Like countless sister organizations nationwide, training and education became a hallmark of the community-based program in Pasadena. Accordingly, Gilmor was instrumental in preparing actors for Hollywood, one exploit that exponentially increased his fame. His educational wing trained actors who became television and film luminaries, like Rue McClanahan, Leonard Nimoy, Dustin Hoffman, Sally Struthers and myriad others. In the 1930s, he became the first person to direct Shakespeare's *Pericles* and the *Henry VI* plays in the United States, thereby also the first to produce the entire body of Shakespeare's thirty-seven plays in America. By 1942, the Pasadena Playhouse had transitioned from an amateur or semi-professional to a professional regional theater. The Playhouse was added in the National Register of Historic Places in 1975 and still actively produces drama as the Official State Theater of California. He attributed his ability to run this theater to his early work in Western Kansas.

Another consequential Hollywood star also kick-started his career in Edwards County. Originally from Portland, Oregon, Don Cook (1901–1961) began his stage career playing a minor role with Kansas City Community Players in a production of *Ambush* in November 1923. Months later, he was cast as the leading man in *Icebound* and *Mary III*. After lead roles in Kinsley, Cook performed again with Charlie in Kansas City before receiving offer after offer, eventually playing with the famed Minnie Maddern Fiske in New York City. Cook had been catapulted to Broadway from Western Kansas and then to an explosively successful Hollywood career in the early 1930s, including *The Public Enemy* (1931), *Safe in Hell*

(1931), *The Spanish Cape Mystery* (1935) and *Show Boat* (1936). He was added to the Hollywood Walk of Fame in 1960.

Two actresses from Kinsley also captured audiences' attention for decades after beginning their careers in their hometown. Lucile DeTar Colyer (1892–1986) launched her performing career unforgettably portraying Shakespeare's Fairy Queen. She then performed in the Santa Fe Reading Rooms with other Kinsley talents. Charlie Edwards enjoyed working with her so much that he selected her as his assistant director for the Arkansas Valley Dramatic Festivals; she then attended Oberlin College and the Juilliard School of Music and performed professionally for decades. Lucile became a classical soprano and performed in various locations, from her beloved hometown to Carnegie Hall. She relocated to West Palm Beach, Florida, in the early 1940s to help her brother manage a three-boat ferry business. In 1964, the gregarious and welcoming Lucile took the helm of her own boat, the *Paddlewheel Queen*. She opened and piloted her four-hundred-passenger dinner cruise boat at age seventy-two, and she remained working on her ship with family until shortly before her death two decades later. In 1912, Lucile famously played Shakespeare's Fairy Queen, and late in life, she again took a similar title, the Ferry Queen.

Likewise, after a breakout performance in the 1912 *Midsummer Night's Dream*, Persis Colie Elsen (1893–1987) continued on a trajectory of performance and instruction for the next several decades. While at the State School for the Deaf in 1922, Colie worked with several other teachers to recover and restage her memories of *A Midsummer Night's Dream*, in which one decade earlier she appeared as the scarlet-clad, mischievous Puck. She took Charlie Edwards's formula even further and organized the play with nearly one thousand students. Despite lifelong troubles with eyesight that led to blindness, Colie maintained her commitment to arts and physical education in the Kansas City region for decades. Out of all of his students, Charlie said that there was not "a finer artist among them than Persis Colie." On that, he and Gilmor Brown agreed. The Pasadena Playhouse director fondly recalled her contributions to his company nearly a half century later.

As the decades passed since Kinsley's stars moved to other locales, people who worked with these luminaries reflected on working with them—particularly in the long-running institutions that continue to produce cultural events. Mrs. Harnsberger, one of Tulsa's lead actresses, reflected on her single season with Kinsley's most renowned director: "Most of us who had not had experience other places learned enough from Charles Edwards to carry us through the next twenty-five years." Unlike the other organizations Charlie founded or served as a director, his last effort, the Tulsa Little Theatre, remained active, serving as a community center for dramatic participation for one hundred years.

In Kinsley, however, the lived memory of the golden age of arts began to fade over time. In 1960, the *Great Bend Tribune* published an article titled "Californian's Death Recalls 'Sylvan Grove' Days at Kinsley," which reflected on Gilmor Brown's and Charlie Edwards's influence on the arts scene. Some people remembered Charlie in Kinsley, but that number was shrinking even then. From his interviews with various individuals, the reporter determined that Charlie "was both loved and misunderstood" at the time. Charlie was a distant memory, and those Shakespeare festivals were a quaint curiosity from the old days.

Maybe some who read this *Great Bend Tribune* article knew that the performance style that Charlie and Gilmor pioneered in Western Kansas had become extremely popular. By this time, communal Shakespeare festivals were not short-lived bandwagons; they had become a significant part of American theater and continue to be in the present day. The artists in Kinsley, Kansas, were among the first ever to create this type of regionally recognized, community-based theater. The eight-column chronicle concluded somberly, "Only the old-timers remember that Kinsley once was the drama capital of the west." However, through the rediscovery of this hidden history, one need not be an "old-timer" to celebrate Kinsley's remarkable contributions to regional arts and literature in the United States.

Selected Bibliography

Alexander, Diane. *Playhouse of the Stars: The Pasadena Playhouse*. Dorleac-MacLeish, 1984.

Arnold, Russell Carl. *The Kansas Inferno: A Study of the Criminal Problem*. Wonderland Publishing Company, 1906.

Baker, George Melville. *Among the Breakers*. George M. Baker & Company, 1876.

Boyd, Josephine Hills. Typewritten unpublished memoir, July 24, 1979. Local history collection, Kinsley Public Library.

Brown, Everett. "Californian's Death Recalls 'Sylvan Grove' Days at Kinsley." *Great Bend (KS) Tribune*, February 7, 1960.

Brown, Gilmor, and Charles Lane. "Pasadena Playhouse Pioneer." Oral History Program, University of California, Los Angeles, 1984.

Bunting, Martha, cousin to Elizabeth Sellers Edwards. Personal diary. Marion Edwards Shouse Lewis Collection, 1896–1933. Unit ID: 474539. Kansas Historical Society Archives.

Burr, Myron C., and Elizabeth Ann Burr, eds. *Kinsley-Edwards County Centennial: From Prairie to People, 1873–1973*. Noland Publishers Inc., 1973.

Busser, Samuel Edwin. *The Santa Fe Reading-Room System*. Atchison, Topeka and Santa Fe Railway Company, 1900. PAM_83159, 83.159, Published Collections Department, Hagley Museum and Library, Wilmington, Delaware.

"Camp Funston." *Symphony in the Flint Hills Field Journal* (2013). https://newprairiepress.org/sfh/2013/folioIII/3.

Centers for Disease Control and Prevention, National Center for Immunization and Respiratory Disease. "History of the 1918 Flu Pandemic." March 21, 2018. https://archive.cdc.gov/www_cdc_gov/flu/pandemic-resources/1918-commemoration/1918-pandemic-history.htm.

Chautard, Emile, dir. *The Mystery of the Yellow Room*. 1919. Mayflower Photoplay Company.

Cloutier, M.M. "A True Ferry Tale." *Palm Beach Daily News*, April 13, 2019.

Edwards, Charles Rufus. Unpublished manuscripts. Marion Edwards Shouse Lewis Collection, 1896–1933. Unit ID: 474539. Kansas Historical Society Archives.

Edwards Family Personal Scrapbook. Local History Collection, Kinsley Public Library.

Hancock-Suran, Irene. "May Williams Ward: Kansas Poet." Master's thesis, Fort Hays State University, 1951.

Henney, Fred. "Brahmin Culture Made Kinsley the 'Athens of the Arkansas Valley'; Greatest Number of Artist Per Acre." *Hutchinson News-Herald*, October 10, 1927.

Hollywood Walk of Fame. "Donald Cook." https://walkoffame.com/donald-cook.

Homan, Delmar C. "Charles Edwards: A Kansas Romantic." Unpublished essay, 2004. Local History Collection, Kinsley Public Library.

———. "Gilmor Brown and Avant-Garde Kansas Theatre, 1912–1916." *Theatre History Studies* 4 (1984): 83–100.

Kinsley High School Annual, 1917. Local History Collection, Kinsley Public Library.

Langer, Lawrence. *The Magic Curtain: The Story of Life in Two Fields, Theatre and Invention, by the Founder of the Theatre Guild.* George G. Harrap and Company, 1952.

Lewandowski, Raymond Joseph. "The Formation, Rise, and Decline of the Tulsa Little Theatre." Dissertation, University of Michigan, 1976.

Lipman, Don. "The Epic B-B-Blizzard that Stranded Hundreds of Well-to-Do Travelers on the Frontier." *Washington Post*, February 5, 2016.

McNamara, Brooks. "The Indian Medicine Show." *Educational Theatre Journal* 23, no. 4 (1971): 431–45.

———. "The Medicine Show Log: Reconstructing a Traditional American Entertainment." *Drama Review: TDR* 28, no. 3 (1984): 74–97.

Miner, Craig. *West of Wichita: Settling the High Plains of Kansas, 1860–1890.* University Press of Kansas, 1995.

Nolan, Leah, and Marybelle Bowman. "The Face of Kansas Still Changing as the Bicentennial Arrives." *Kansas Quarterly* 8, no. 2 (Spring 1976): 89–93.

Punahou Archives. "History of Punahou." https://www.punahou.edu/archives/history-of-punahou.

Rhoads, Jane Glotfelty. *Kansas Opera Houses: Actors and Community Events, 1855–1925.* Mennonite Press Inc., 2008.

Richardson, Myrtle H. *Changes Road to the Winds: A History of Edwards County*. Lewis Press Inc., 1986.

———. *Great Next Year Country: A History of Edwards County*. Lewis Press Inc., 1983.

———. *Oft' Told Tales: A History of Edwards County*. Lewis Press Inc., 1976.

Shortridge, James R. *Peopling the Plains: Who Settled Where in Frontier Kansas.* University Press of Kansas, 1995.

Shoup, Gail Leo, Jr. *The Pasadena Community Playhouse: Its Origins and History from 1917 to 1942*. Dissertation, University of California–Los Angeles, 1968.
Shouse, Marion Edwards. Personal scrapbook. Edwards County Historical Society.
Stauffer, Suzanne M. "Correct Provision Can Be Made for Their Wants: The Reading Rooms of the Santa Fe Railroad." *Library & Information History* 39 (2023): 1–22.
Thies, Randall M. "Civil War Valor in Concrete: David A. Lester and the Kinsley Civil War Monument." *Kansas History* 22 (Autumn 1999): 164–81.
Thomas, David G. *Dirty Dave Rudabaugh, Billy the Kid's Most Feared Companion*. Mesilla Valley History Series, Doc 45 Publishing, 2023.
Ward, May William. *No Two Years Alike*. Triangle Publishing Company, 1961.
Wolfgang, William Floyd. "Grassroots Shakespeare: 'I Love Shakespeare, and I Live Here': Amateur Shakespeare Performance in American Communities." *Shakespeare Bulletin* 39, no. 3 (2021): 355–73.

A Note on Newspaper Sources

The majority of the histories in this book have either been drawn directly from local newspaper sources or, at the very least, supported by them. For direct quotes, we have provided the edition of that paper directly in the text, but for other sourced material, one can find the events recorded on the given date in the following local newspapers. Other newspapers that are cited are directly referenced in the text itself.

Edwards County Leader (Kinsley, KS), 1877–80.
Kinsley (KS) Daily Mercury, 1887–88.
Kinsley (KS) Graphic, 1878–1925.
Kinsley (KS) Mercury, 1883–1925.
Kinsley (KS) Reporter, 1876–77.
Kinsley (KS) Republican, 1878–81.
Valley Republican (Kinsley, KS), 1877–80.

Index

D

E

F

G

H

J

K

L

M

N

O

P

R

About the Authors

Joan K. Weaver recently retired as the director of the Kinsley Public Library in Kinsley, Kansas. For the past twenty-eight years, she has worked to discover, preserve and make the stories of this prairie community digitally accessible through the library website and blog. She has conducted eighty-five oral histories of local citizens, which capture life in Edwards County from the Dust Bowl days through World War II. Originally from Michigan, she earned her degree from Eastern Michigan University and spent many years teaching English, speech and drama in Michigan, New Mexico and Kansas. She enjoys telling the stories of people through historical characters, essays and poetry.

William Floyd Wolfgang, PhD, is a lecturer in English literature and the Director of Service Scholars at Stevenson University in Owings Mills, Maryland. He is also a theater practitioner in York, Pennsylvania, where he produced nearly the entire Shakespearean canon with the OrangeMite Shakespeare Company. After serving as a special researcher at the Shakespeare Birthplace Trust in the United Kingdom, he completed the first major study of community-based Shakespeare performance in the United States. Dr. Wolfgang has published research on related topics in various collections and journals. For the last six years, his studies have taken him to Kinsley, Kansas, where he continues uncovering early twentieth-century Shakespeare festivals and community-based arts.